MAKING ZEN YOUR OWN

MAKING ZEN YOUR OWN

GIVING LIFE TO TWELVE KEY GOLDEN AGE ANCESTORS

JANET JIRYU ABELS

WISDOM PUBLICATIONS · BOSTON

Wisdom Publications
199 Elm Street
Somerville MA 02144 USA
www.wisdompubs.org

Library of Congress Cataloging-in-Publication Data

Abels, Janet Jiryu.
  Making Zen your own : giving life to Zen's golden age ancestors / Janet Jiryu Abels.
    p. cm.
  Includes bibliographical references.
  ISBN 0-86171-702-3 (pbk. : alk. paper)
  1. Zen priests—China—Biography. 2. Zen Buddhism—Doctrines. I. Title.
BQ9298.A23 2012
294.3'9270922—dc23
[B]
                                    2011030587

ISBN 9780861717026
eBook ISBN 9781614290292

16 15 14 13 12
5   4   3   2   1

The map on page 179 in the appendix is by Andy Ferguson. The lineage chart on page 180 in the appendix is by Frank Lo Cicero. Author photo on page 189 is by Mark Rubin. Cover design by Phil Pascuzzo. Interior design by Gopa&Ted2. Set in ScalaPro 10.25/14.5.

Wisdom Publications' books are printed on acid-free paper and meet the guidelines for permanence and durability of the Production Guidelines for Book Longevity of the Council on Library Resources.

Printed in the United States of America.

This book was produced with environmental mindfulness. We have elected to print this title on 30% PCW recycled paper. As a result, we have saved the following resources: 12 trees, 5 million BTUs of energy, 1,225 lbs. of greenhouse gases, 5,526 gallons of water, and 350 lbs. of solid waste. For more information, please visit our website, www.wisdompubs.org. This paper is also FSC certified. For more information, please visit www.fscus.org.

To my daughter, Carrie,
without whose help this book
would never have been written

Contents

Introduction

A GENERIC ZEN MASTER on a mountain top—when I began doing koan work in my formative years of Zen training, this is how I generally perceived the Chinese Zen masters whose paradoxical teachings I was trying to break open. All the major Zen koans are based on the insights of Chinese teachers who lived primarily between the sixth and tenth centuries. These teachers were, for me, shadowy figures with strange names—sometimes Chinese, sometimes Japanese, depending on which source I was reading—and they were seemingly devoid of individuality, life history, and societal context. To be sure, there was biographical material on them in the various koan books I was using, largely presented in the commentaries on the koans, written by modern Zen masters. But the biographies didn't mean much to me, since I knew little about Chinese history and geography and had no interest then in finding out more because—well, working through the koans was hard enough.

All of this began to change as I moved more deeply into koan study and especially after I began to teach. In the spring of 2001, faced with the daunting task as a new teacher of having to write four talks for the annual weeklong summer retreat of New York City–based Still Mind Zendo, which I founded and where I am now co-resident teacher, I hit upon the idea of focusing on just one of the Chinese masters who had appeared in the koan texts I had worked on. The first one I chose was the ninth-century master Deshan Xuanjian (J. Tokusan Senkan), because the koans that came out of his teachings seemed to reveal an interesting figure. I decided to present Deshan's insights in the context of his life story, which I pieced together from biographies in the koan texts and personal research—and then filled in a bit using my imagination. I connected Deshan's teachings and life story to the practice challenges and life issues faced by those attending the retreat at which I was teaching about him. In subsequent years I chose a different Chinese master for each of my summer retreat talks, and it is these talks that I have adapted into this book. Accordingly, though grounded in the facts as known by scholars, I encourage the reader to meet this book not as a work of scholarship but as Zen teaching expressed through the life stories of these ancestors.

What I discovered is that these men (and sadly, it is indeed only men who are represented in what has for centuries been the official Zen record) were not formed from a generic mold but individuals with interesting quirks, senses of humor, heartfelt enlightenment experiences, varied ways of living, and unique ways of expressing the Dharma. In other words I discovered that they were each *human*. I discovered, for example, that Dajian Huineng (J. Daikan Eno) was an animal rights advocate of sorts; that Mazu Daoyi (J. Baso Doitsu) had a rough-and-tumble personality; that Shitou Xiqian (J. Sekito Kisen) had been a hermit for a large part of his life; that Deshan, in his early years, was a man of high drama. I learned that Zhaozhou Congshen (J. Joshu Jushin), enlightened at an early age, did not become the master of his own (miserably cold) monastery until well into his eighties; that Linji Yixuan (J. Rinzai Gigen), later known for exploding all the "Zen rules," had been in his early years a strict fundamentalist; and that Xuefeng Yicun (J. Seppo Gison) had been an utter failure as a Zen student. Yes! I discovered that these men were human, not the rarified, superhuman beings I had always imagined them to be. And I discovered that it was their humanity that could teach us as much as the words they spoke. It was their humanity that brought their teachings to life, gave the teachings freshness, and, above all, offered encouragement. Being familiar with their humanity allowed me to know with confidence that if they could do it, so can I, so can you—so can we! Isn't that what Zen encouragement is all about? These great teachers have all certainly encouraged me. They opened and continue to open my limited vision. They taught me and continue to teach me about different ways of seeing into the true nature of reality. They strengthened and continue to strengthen my determination and my practice.

Knowing the life stories of these masters not only enriched my experience of their teaching but also sparked a deeper understanding of their social and political environments, as well as their connection to one another. The Dharma, after all, is not a static entity. It is life, and just like life, the Dharma evolves in the context of the times in which it is practiced and builds on all that came before. So it is important to know, for example, that Zen was greatly influenced by the nature-based, Chinese *Tao te Ching* and the ethical teachings of Confucius, that it began to be formalized during a brutal and savage period of strife in Chinese history, and that in many ways the Dharma of Shakyamuni Buddha in the fourth century BCE was not the same as the Dharma in China more than a thousand years later—although both point to the heart of the Great Matter of life and death. It was expressed differently a thousand years later, because the Dharma, while fundamentally unchanged, is always changing and always evolving.

In addition, just as it is important for Americans to know that Lincoln came after Washington, Jefferson, and Madison, and was influenced by each, it is important for us as Zen practitioners to know that Mazu preceded Linji, that Zhaozhou was Mazu's Dharma grandson, and that Huineng was the Zen ancestor of us all. For just as Lincoln evolved from—and used—the insights of Washington, Jefferson, and Madison, each Zen ancestor built upon the insights of those who came before. Tracing how these interconnections and linkages developed from generation to generation of Chinese teachers offers today's Zen practitioner invaluable context. Knowing, for instance, that Huineng's "not one thing exists" led to Mazu's "ordinary mind is the Way," which led to Zhaozhou's famous *Mu*, helps us to see more clearly into the essence of *Mu*, the first koan in the book of koans known as *The Gateless Gate* (*Wumenguan* in Chinese and *Mumonkan* in Japanese). It also helps us to see that our *own* insight is born out of this unbroken line of Zen

Buddhist teachers and that we—yes, we—are also part of the evolving Dharma.

Knowing the history of our Zen ancestors—knowing what difficulties and obstacles they overcame in order to see clearly, being aware of their intense determination and unrelenting discipline, understanding their relationships with one another, seeing the uniqueness of each one's teaching, knowing a little about the times they lived in—is, it seems to me, indispensable for anyone seriously interested in Zen. Grasping the essence of any koan or Zen teaching is greatly helped by knowing who the person was who originally expressed that teaching. The great teachers of the ages are appreciated far more when we know their history. Jesus did not teach in a generic land during some vague period; he taught in a particular land at a particular time. The same can be said for Shakyamuni Buddha. In modern times, we must place Gandhi in modern-day India and Martin Luther King Jr. in the American Deep South in order to appreciate their insights. Why should this not be true of the great Zen ancestors?

We miss so much when we disembody the Zen masters, reducing them only to their preserved teachings. More significantly, we run the risk of separating the insights of the Zen ancestors from our own lives if we separate the ancestors from theirs. "Zen is your life. Appreciate your life," taught Taizan Maezumi Roshi, the founder of the White Plum Asanga. And indeed Zen *was* life for these teachers. Not to know about their lives is to miss a great deal of their splendid Dharma.

I BEGIN THIS BOOK with the four foundational masters whose teachings made Zen what it is today: Bodhidharma, Huineng, Mazu, and Shitou. The first, Bodhidharma, was an Indian Buddhist monk who early in the sixth century brought the essence of meditation, or *chan* (*zen* in Japanese), to China. His history is murky, often shrouded in legend, and key dates in his life are uncertain, but recent discoveries by Zen scholars such as Andy Ferguson and modern Chinese researchers are revealing more clues that seem to contradict the popularly accepted version of Bodhidharma's life. A thirteenth-century text has him arriving in China as a rather elderly man in 527 and meeting with Emperor

Wu—a famous encounter at the heart of Zen Buddhist lore—shortly after that. However, the earliest record, *Continued Biographies of Eminent Monks*, has Bodhidharma arriving in China on or before the year 475, a date that some scholars say is more reliable since, according to Ferguson, *Continued Biographies* was written "perhaps only 130 years or so after Bodhidharma lived." Under this scenario, Bodhidharma could not have met the emperor upon his arrival, since Wu did not ascend the throne until 502. Instead, it would have taken place at a later date. I base my chapter on this timeline because it makes the most sense to me.

Skipping four generations of teachers whose recorded history is slim, I come to Huineng, the great sixth patriarch, out of whom, it is said, all Zen flows. His personal story and teaching are compiled in what is known as the Platform Sutra, a work that modern scholarship has pretty much determined was written by one of his disciples after the master's death. His life is described in embellished, almost mythic, terms in the richly detailed biography that opens the work, but myths hold much truth, and his story, as recounted by the monk who wrote it, contains splendid teaching, while the purported lectures of the master that make up the bulk of the text remain part of Zen's fundamental teachings. The Platform Sutra made Huineng a deeply respected figure in not only Zen Buddhism but Tibetan Buddhism as well, and later generations of Chinese teachers traced all Zen lines back to him.

Huineng's Dharma grandsons, Mazu and Shitou, each spawned successors who were to develop what came to be known later as the Five Schools of Zen, two of which exist to this day: the Linji (J. Rinzai) school, formed by Mazu's Dharma great-grandson Linji, and the Caodong (J. Soto) school, formed by Shitou's Dharma great-grandson Dongshan Lingjie (J. Tozan Ryokai). Three other masters described in this book developed such distinctive ways of teaching that they were designated as founders of Zen schools that carried their names, though these schools eventually died out as their teachings were absorbed into the Rinzai and Soto schools. The founders of these three schools are Guishan Lingyou (J. Isan Reiyu), Fayan Wenyi (J. Hogen Bun'eki), and Yunmen Wenyan (J. Ummon Bun'en).

Deshan is part of the story not only because Yunmen and Fayan, as well as Xuefeng (whose early years of "failing" at Zen offer us much encouragement), were all his Dharma descendants, but also because Deshan was a colorful personality, to say the least. Finally, no book on the Golden Age Zen masters would be complete without Zhaozhou, another great-grandson of Mazu, because of the depth and breadth of his insight. Zhaozhou has twenty koans in the The Gateless Gate and The Blue Cliff Record alone; his teachings survived, even though he did not found a Zen school, because of their directness and simplicity.

I have touched on the lives and teachings of twelve masters. But it is my hope that being introduced to some of Zen's Chinese ancestors in this way will encourage readers to approach other ancestors in a similar fashion—to take what is known of their lives and imagine what was not recorded. There are several excellent sources one can use, but Andy Ferguson's book Zen's Chinese Heritage certainly stands out. While I examine only a few of the major figures of Zen's Chinese years, Ferguson presents all of them and provides fine samples of their teachings. In addition, The Roaring Stream, edited by Nelson Foster and Jack Shoemaker, is another collection of writings by the major Chinese masters that offers today's practitioners easy access to their teachings.

Finally, this book is based on scholarly sources and historical records, but most of these historical records do not necessarily present historical facts in the way we think of facts. The early records of the Chinese masters were written by others to preserve and pass on the *essence* of a particular teacher, primarily the essence of his teaching. Biography was not an important concern and, as such, played a minor role in the records. In addition, biographical details were not always factual and were often tailored to fit a particular Zen master after he had passed away. What was important to the biographer was the essence of his subject and the subject's teaching. It would be helpful for the reader to approach these teachers in the same way.

To tie this book together, I have intertwined Dharma reflections of my own, based on my years as a Zen student and a Zen teacher. The result, I hope, is a presentation of Zen insight vividly relevant for the twenty-first century, addressing both the needs of longtime Zen practitioners and those new to the way of Zen. Knowing that it is easier to digest and retain information that comes through storytelling, I have strived to present the history and teaching of each ancestor as a story and, in this way, to bring each of these seminal masters to life in such a way that their teachings can be heard afresh, with new ears.

For me, these great teachers are no longer generic Zen masters on a mountain top. Rather, they are now my friends, fellow travelers, and above all encouragers in the Dharma, whom I have grown not only to know and respect but also to love. It is my hope that readers of this book will come to see them in the same way.

In light of all this, I can say quite certainly that the Chinese Zen masters are alive and well and teaching today.

1. BODHIDHARMA

NO KNOWING STANDS HERE

ZEN IS ABOUT EXPLORATION of the unknown. It is about leaving the safety of one's accumulated mind-based knowledge and its sense of certainty, and moving ever so slowly into the unknowable, unimaginable experience of "absolute" or "essential" reality, which is none other than one's very self. Exploration of the unknown is never easy, whether it is physical travel to a new land, psychological travel into the complex layers of one's psyche, or travel into the limitless mystery of one's essential self. It requires a strong sense of longing to find or realize "something other" than that which is familiar. It requires willpower, focus, discipline, and determination. It requires facing fears and proceeding regardless. It requires faith. It requires resolve.

Such an exploration, then, such a journey, could have no better metaphor than the sea voyage undertaken by the man who brought the essence of what came to be called Chan (*Zen* in Japanese) from India to China. His name is Bodhidharma, and though his history is unclear, one characteristic seems to stand out: Bodhidharma did not turn away from the unknown—he sailed right into it.

The earliest record tells us that around the year 475, a Buddhist monk in his early thirties, born into privilege as the son of an Indian rajah, crossed the sea from India to China. Bodhidharma's voyage took three years. Nothing much has been written by scholars about this voyage, primarily because there is very little documentation of it, but we have the freedom to look at the trip imaginatively and learn a great deal from it for our own journey of self-discovery. Lacking details, it is easy to have the impression that Bodhidharma sailed across effortlessly and without challenge. But did he? What about perilous seas, pirates, unfamiliar languages, strange lands, and different customs? Who was there in China to encourage him? There were no teachers around, no family, and no servants. He was young and he was alone. Was he scared? Did he feel lost? It is hard to imagine that he did not. Could romantic visions that he might have formed in India about the Buddha Way have crashed mightily on such a journey? Could he have had doubts about his desire to bring the essence of the Dharma to China, doubts about his capability to carry it out, and perhaps even doubts about the Dharma itself? Surely he must have lost his compass more than once. One is reminded of Andre Gide's words: "In order to discover new lands, one must be willing to lose sight of the shore for a very long time."

Bodhidharma surely lost sight of the shore, both literally and figuratively, for a very long time. Do we lose sight on *our* journeys of self-discovery? Are there not times when we too feel lost, alone, and scared? Is our faith in, and our longing for, an intangible "something" often battered by doubt? Don't our romantic visions of enlightenment often become confused? If so, perhaps we can find determination and resolve in Bodhidharma's journey across the sea. Perhaps we can find in his journey the courage to steer ourselves ever deeper into the perilous waters of our own particular unknowns, just as he did. Bodhidharma did not turn back, even though he did not know what lay ahead. And for us, the sooner we discover the fruits of moving forward through the unknowns of our own explorations—accepting that true awakening is never an easy journey—the sooner turning back will become impossible.

Recent scholarly discoveries, as well as the earliest records, indicate that Bodhidharma was born around the year 440 in the southern Indian kingdom of Palava. He was a member of the warrior class, the third son of the ruler of that kingdom, and at a young age he developed a deep interest in the Buddha Way. This is why his father invited the great Mahayana Buddhist teacher Prajnatara, the twenty-seventh Indian ancestor of the Zen lineage, to travel from the northeastern Buddhist heartland of Magadah to instruct his son.

Prajnatara's name means "pearl of wisdom," and he had received that name from his own teacher because of his deep insight into the nonduality, or Oneness, of all that exists. He had realized that essential or absolute reality is One, and that this One is expressed as everything, experienced as everything. We, then, are not separate from One—it is us. In "just this moment" we are complete—all we have to do is realize this startling truth. Now, these are encouraging words for those of us who long to discover who we really are, as they no doubt were for the young prince. We don't *become* the reality or truth of who we are. Rather, we awaken to the truth of who we *already* are, a truth hidden from us by our ignorant ego-mind. Such awakening cannot be *understood* with this ego-mind, it can only be *experienced* when that mind is still, when all separations (or discriminations as Zen calls them) drop away and we fully realize that everything, including our ignorant ego-mind, is one essential reality. As Bodhidharma later wrote in a work attributed to him called the Bloodstream Sermon, "to search for enlightenment or nirvana beyond this mind is impossible." In other words, Oneness is not something outside of us—it *is* us.

This is the *prajna*, or wisdom, that Prajnatara allowed to rise up in his gifted student, letting him proceed slowly until he had grasped the principle of nonduality for himself and awakened to the truth. After this awakening, the young prince requested ordination as a Buddhist monk and received the name Bodhidharma ("Awakened Teaching"). Prajnatara then encouraged him to leave India and bring his innate wisdom and noble spirit to the vast regions of China. So it was that Bodhidharma left his homeland and set out for unknown lands to the northeast. He sailed from the southern port of Mahabalipuram, traveling across the Indian Ocean (at that time the overland route between India and China was blocked by the Huns), with presumed stops at various ports in such modern-day countries as Burma, Thailand, Malaysia, and Cambodia. He arrived in China around the year 475.

AT THIS TIME, Buddhism in China was thriving, having been brought from India through overland routes during the first century. In the northern kingdom, more than five thousand Buddhist temples flourished, while in the southern kingdom there were about two thousand. Emphasis in these early years of Buddhism in China was on doctrines, philosophical discussion, rituals, the building of monasteries, and the copying and translating of texts, although meditation, the heart of the Buddha Way, was certainly practiced and taught by these early monks. The Indian "Sutra on Concentration by Practicing Respiratory Exercises" was translated into Chinese during the second century, and *chan* became the Chinese character for the Sanskrit word *dhyana* (meditation), though the popular notion of meditation was that it produced magical powers.

The Chinese were especially attracted to the wisdom teachings (the Prajnaparamita sutras) of Mahayana Buddhism. A major reason for this was that these teachings found special affinity with the Chinese wisdom of the Tao te Ching of Lao Tzu (written about a thousand years earlier, around the time of Siddhartha Gautama, the Buddha) and the writings of the fourth-century sage Chuang Tzu. It is easy to see this affinity because even today the Tao resonates strongly with Zen practitioners. Heinrich Dumoulin, in an excellent chapter on early Buddhism in China in his book *Zen Buddhism: A History, India and China*, also tells us that the naturalistic spirit of Taoism found deep connection with the Mahayanist sutras (Buddhist scriptures). "Where the Indians had been inhibited by their agonizing struggle for salvation, the Chinese, who desired nothing so much as to penetrate the secrets of nature, were attracted to Taoist-Buddhist naturalism." All in all, Buddhism and Taoism connected. As Dumoulin writes, "The fusion of Mahayana metaphysics and the Chinese view of life was so complete that the borderlines between influence and originality can no longer be clearly defined."

So this is the China in which Bodhidharma landed when he arrived at the southern port of Nanhai somewhere around 475, with his teaching of "pointing to mind." Being Indian, he must have stood out among the Chinese teachers, not only because he looked different and was a Buddhist from India, the country of Buddhism's origin, but also because the Dharma he spoke about must have sounded so extreme. Bodhidharma taught direct experience of absolute reality, while the Chinese

Buddhist teachers were primarily concerned with philosophical discussion *about* absolute reality.

Virtually nothing definitive is known about Bodhidharma's activities during his early years in China. Presumably he took time to learn Chinese and become accustomed to his new landscape, but what happened to him during the first fifteen or twenty years in his adopted country is unclear. One thing does stand out, however: he seems to have been extraordinarily patient. I mean, if you were sent on a mission by your revered teacher, could you spend up to twenty years in obscurity without trying to *do* something—without trying to become well known, trying to find students, trying to get a *publicist*? (Bodhidharma probably did teach during this time, but since no record of such teaching exists we can assume his teaching was not very extensive, or at least it didn't take hold in people.) What an example this period of his life can set for us. It shows us that we too must learn to develop patience and not be in a hurry; that we do not need results in order to trust that we are on the right path; that we too must develop confidence in ourselves by simply being open, being attentive, and allowing events to unfold in their own time—which, after all, is the only time in which they can unfold. But all this is difficult, for to live this way is to live counter to immense societal forces that constantly demand from us immediate success, immediate results, with no room allowed for slow maturation. It takes courage, confidence, and sheer determination not to get sucked under by such forces, and that is why the discipline that Zen offers is essential.

The first indication we have of Bodhidharma's whereabouts after his arrival in China is from *Continued Biographies of Eminent Monks*, a seventh-century text by the monk Dao Xuan, which placed him near the northern kingdom city of Luoyang between the years 485 and 497. (As noted in the introduction to this book, recent scholarly discoveries by Andy Ferguson and others offer a possible account of Bodhidharma's activities from this time on; it is this account I will be following for the rest of this chapter.) During this time, tradition says Bodhidharma chose to live among "peaks and caves" on nearby Mount Song, the central peak of China's sacred mountains. Perhaps this is because, as Ferguson surmises, he feared the Buddhist establishment, which was closely allied to the northern imperial court, and which did not look kindly on iconoclastic teachers. Some Buddhist and Taoist temples already existed on Mount Song (although not, as is widely held, Shaolin Temple—still active to this day—which was not built until a decade later), but Bodhidharma did not join them. Rather, he chose to live for six years (some texts say nine) on Mount Song, in a cave facing a wall, thus becoming known as the Indian Brahmin Who Faces a Wall.

Bodhidharma is well known for this wall facing, but the significance of his choice to do this can easily elude us, given the context of his mission from his teacher. This Indian brahmin, this holy man, sat facing a wall for six years—and that is all he did. He didn't work at getting a name for himself or developing a profile or getting influence. The confidence of his choice is almost breathtaking. And just what *was* this "wall facing"? What was he doing? He was *doing* nothing—other than disappearing, so to speak, allowing his ignorant ego-mind to drop off. Once again, he was opening into the unknown—just as he had done when he chose to leave his homeland. Such risk-taking, leaving the safety of mental certainties for exploration of the unknown, is the true work of meditation, for it is the only way one can realize one's essential reality. But does one have to be in a cave to face a wall? Does one even have to have a wall to face a wall? What is it that one faces when one faces the wall? Who is it facing the wall? And just what *is* the wall? These questions are up to each of us to resolve.

Bodhidharma did, however, attract some attention. Buddhist and Taoist seekers came to these mountains and some of them were eventually drawn to him. His first documented disciple was a man named Seng Fu who stayed with him until sometime around 495, at which time Seng Fu moved south to Nanjing. Bodhidharma's other known student, Huike, was the man who would become the second Chinese patriarch (for although Bodhidharma was an Indian, he is considered to be the first Chinese patriarch). Huike had assiduously studied Buddhist teachings but he was still not satisfied. Even after many years of searching— he was into middle age by this time—something was still not resolved for Huike. And here he models for us another basic Zen tenet: we must seek, we must practice, and we must strive, until we resolve the Great

Matter, as Zen calls it. Someone else's resolution (often presented in the form of books and lectures) will not suffice. Through determined Zen practice we must each resolve the Great Matter of life and death for ourselves, no matter how long it takes. And that is why Huike's awakening, as tradition tells it, is so encouraging. It is one of the great Zen stories of all time. It is perhaps the ultimate Zen story of determination.

In his search, Huike heard of the wall-gazing brahmin from India and traveled to Bodhidharma's cave on Mount Song. But Bodhidharma wanted nothing of this seeker. Even though it was a cold and snowy day in December, Bodhidharma would not let him enter, calling out to Huike that he, Huike, was shallow and arrogant, with little wisdom—in other words, not up to the task. Bodhidharma sure was a tough fellow, wasn't he? No wonder he had virtually no disciples. But he had met his match, for Huike was equally tough. As he stood, rejected, shivering in the snow, he took a knife and cut off his arm to show how he would do anything to awaken—and, the story goes, his blood dripped on the white snow. On seeing this, Bodhidharma realized the man's strength and resolve, and accepted him as his student.

Zen is hard. To wake up to the truth of who we really are is difficult. Many people come to this practice with great enthusiasm, but when they begin to see how challenging it is, they say, "this is not what I bargained for," and, sadly, walk away. Realization cannot happen without a strong desire to awaken and it cannot happen without sacrifice. Only one who has struggled with his or her own inner torments can fully appreciate Huike's intense and desperate need to see clearly. The teaching here is that such intense need must be there and it can only be fulfilled through struggle and sacrifice. To die to self, which is what waking up is all about, means that metaphorically our blood, just as Huike's, must be spilled on fresh snow. Dying to self so that we can see clearly is very painful. How intense is *your* need to see clearly?

Once in front of the master, Huike pinpointed the source of his angst, angst so intense that he had been willing to cut off his arm. He said, "I have studied, I have read, I have dedicated myself to becoming awake, but my mind is not yet at peace. Bring me peace, master." In other words: "Something doesn't fit. There is still a hole inside of me.

I am not complete. Help me." And Bodhidharma replied: "Well, bring me your mind and I will set it at peace." What a brilliant response. He didn't deny the mind, and he didn't deny the torment, the truth of Huike's experience of not being at peace. Like the Buddha, Bodhidharma approached the problem scientifically: "Bring me your mind," he said, "and I will set it at peace." So Huike set about looking, really exhaustively searching, for his mind. After some time he came back and said, "I've searched everywhere for my mind but my mind is unfindable." "Then," said Bodhidharma, "I have set it at peace."

Huike stayed with his teacher for eight years. He became the second Chinese Zen patriarch, spending most of his rather obscure life teaching in the streets of the capital city, Yedu, and eventually passing on the Dharma (teaching) to his student Sengcan, who became the third Chinese patriarch in the Zen lineage.

"My mind is not at peace. Please bring me peace."

What about you? Are you also seeking to put your mind at peace? Are you trying to outrun something, change something, become something, achieve something, know something, awaken to something? Is your mind, too, not at peace? Why not follow Bodhidharma's advice? Look for your mind. What do you find? Do you find your mind? Or do you find "just this"?

AROUND 495, the emperor of the northern kingdom moved his court to Luoyang and soon after began the construction of Shaolin Temple on Mount Song. This seems to have been the catalyst for the anti-institutional Bodhidharma to leave his cave, cross the Yangtze River (on a reed, tradition tells us) and move to the southern kingdom, possibly to be near his disciple Seng Fu in Nanjing, capital of the Qi dynasty that ruled in the south. It was during this time that the famous meeting between Bodhidharma and Emperor Wu (which comes to us as the first koan in *The Blue Cliff Record*) probably took place. Emperor Wu had ascended the throne of southern China in 502 and, according to Andy Ferguson, "his long rule, from 502–549, saw an intimate connection between Buddhism and the imperial throne hardly matched by any other era of Chinese history." Though Ferguson opens up the possibility that Wu may have used Buddhism to enhance his imperial power, there is no doubt that he was an ardent Buddhist. He "lived in a single room without furniture at the rear of the palace, sleeping on a plain mat on the ground, spending much of his time studying the scriptures." He supported Buddhist monasteries, built temples, and had texts translated. Bodhidharma's radical teaching surely must have come to his attention, and this is why the Indian monk was invited for an audience at court—though why Bodhidharma decided to shake off his distrust of power and accept the invitation is unclear. Perhaps his disciple Seng Fu persuaded him to go, or perhaps he saw that the emperor's interest in Buddhism was genuine. No matter, the important thing is that he went. The meeting has become part of Buddhist lore.

As the story goes, Bodhidharma stood before the emperor, who said to him: "Since coming to the throne, I've had temples built, sutras translated, monks ordained. Tell me, what merit have I gained?" "No merit at all," replied Bodhidharma. What astonishment that must have caused—to stand in front of the emperor and tell him he had gained no merit. The twelfth-century commentary on this in *The Blue Cliff Record* says: "He threw dirty water on the emperor right away." To his great credit, the emperor did not have Bodhidharma thrown out, but asked, "Why no merit?" This was a legitimate question, since "merit" for one's good deeds was very much part of the Buddhist teaching the emperor had been taught. "These works of merit are all illusions and are not real," Bodhidharma replied. Again, the emperor must have been stopped in his tracks but continued to remain engaged. He asked a logical question: "So what is the meaning, then, of the holy truths?" Bodhidharma replied: "Vast emptiness. Nothing holy." Dumbfounded, the emperor asked, "Who is this who stands before me?" "I don't know," was the reply.

Let's examine this famous exchange, for it offers parallels for our own lives. "What merit have I gained?" Surely this is a familiar question for us, as well as the emperor. If I sit in meditation, if I put in my hours, if I do service at the zendo, if I study, if I work on koans, if I impress the teacher, I will surely gain something, right? I will surely achieve something, right? No, I will not gain or achieve anything: no gain, no merit. So then we might ask, "If there is nothing to gain, why do it at all?

Why go through all this Zen madness? Why sit? Why practice?" And there is no answer that anyone can give us, only the answer we arrive at on our own, just as Emperor Wu was left to determine his own answer for himself. How do we find our answer, though? By practicing *zazen*, or sitting meditation. There is no other way. For it is only through the practice of stilling the mind through meditation that we can answer the questions that Bodhidharma's responses raise. As *The Blue Cliff Record* says, "If you can grasp this statement 'no merit' you can meet Bodhidharma face to face." "What, then, is the holy teaching?" we ask, along with the emperor. "What is it that I'm supposed to be seeking? What is holiness, what is goodness, what is the mystery?" No holiness, no teaching, no goodness, no mystery, Bodhidharma ultimately tells us. Just emptiness. "But what is emptiness?" The only way to find out is to practice and realize that it is *everything*.

The emperor was truly at a loss after asking about the holy truths, so he demanded, "Who are you?" Bodhidharma replied, "I don't know," or, as Katsuki Sekida Roshi says is the correct translation, "No knowing. No knowing stands here." Now, "no knowing" has to be true "no knowing," not just a concept that makes sense intellectually but is not lived out and therefore entangles us more. We should not make "no knowing" into another idea the way we tend to make "enlightenment" into an idea that we have to then smash to pieces. So the "I don't know" that we so regularly say in frustration when we practice Zen—"I don't know why I'm doing this," "I don't know what this means"—is necessary. "I don't know" or "I don't understand" is *the entry point* into the "not-knowing" of Zen. It is the letting go of our mental entanglements, and we must begin to trust this truth whenever we become frustrated. It is easy to put ourselves down when we don't "get it," as if there were something wrong with us. But there is nothing wrong with us. Confusion, turbulence, and doubt are all part of the not-knowing of Zen.

Through his insight and practice, Bodhidharma had developed the confidence to stand in front of an emperor and say "I don't know" because *he really did not know*. The mind, which creates "knowing," was completely still as he stood there. But a still mind is not a dead mind, or an ignorant mind. It is an alive mind—just one that doesn't know. So if you're confused, if you don't know what you're doing, if you feel dumb or stupid when you're engaged in Zen practice, learn to trust it. Strange as it may seem, *this* is the Way—the awakening way. Don't change course. Keep sitting in not-knowing with the strength of a Bodhidharma, all the time seeking to realize no merit.

After the exchange with Emperor Wu, Bodhidharma left the court, but according to the commentary in *The Blue Cliff Record*, the emperor remained intrigued. Perhaps he intuited something about that "I don't know." He asked Master Chi, one of the monks at court, "Who was that man who stood before me?" And Master Chi answered, "This is the Bodhisattva of Compassion directly transmitting the mind of Buddha." The emperor felt regret and was going to send an emissary to bring Bodhidharma back.

But truly, was there anyone to "bring back"?

BODHIDHARMA SEEMS TO HAVE stayed on in the southern kingdom for some years, but then at some point returned to the north. According to Huike's biography in *Continued Biographies*, Bodhidharma died on the banks of the Luo River in the year 528 but, as Andy Ferguson writes, "Any conclusion about Bodhidharma's final days and place of death remains very speculative." An enigma to the end, he died, his essence now awakened in a middle-aged, one-armed Chinese man who passed on the Dharma in the streets with the same resolve and determination as his teacher until his own death in 593 at the age of 107. In *The Transmission of the Lamp*, Tao-yuan records Bodhidharma's prophecy, the five-petal reference being to the future five schools of Zen:

> I came to this land originally to transmit the Dharma
> And to bring deliverance from error.
> A flower opens five petals
> The fruit ripens of itself.

Looked at as a whole, then, what did Bodhidharma do? From the perspective of oneness, he did nothing. Everything is complete already. The fruit ripens of itself. Even from the relative point of view, he didn't seem to achieve very much. Yet how like our journey is his journey. He awakened through teaching—so must we. He studied, he practiced—so must we. He took an arduous journey, far from the safety of the shore—so must we. He came to a foreign land, the land of not-knowing—so must we. He stood up to outer authority—so must we. He sat, in discipline, facing a wall, facing his unknowns, his limitations, his vastness, and his boundlessness—so must we. He taught the Dharma by embodying it—so must we. He passed away—so must we.

He passed away with no sangha, no buildings, no followers, no fame, no success, just unbridled confidence in the Dharma of not-knowing. And out of this thin reed of seeming failure, Zen flourished. What teaching and inspiration for us who always have to know the outcome before we take even the smallest step, who continually base everything on results, on how things look, who need titles and positions and acknowledgment, who don't dare take risks, who can't bear to let go of our safety nets. What teaching and inspiration!

However, the final teaching of this man's life, strangely enough, might have come from Emperor Wu, who mourned Bodhidharma's death and personally wrote an inscription for his monument:

> Alas, I saw him without seeing him.
> I met him without meeting him.
> I encountered him without encountering him.
> Now, as before, I regret this deeply.

Who do *we* see without seeing? Who do *we* meet without meeting? What do *we* encounter without encountering? Do we regret this deeply? And if we do, what are we going to do about it?

Where is Bodhidharma right now? Wake up! Bodhidharma is sitting on *your* cushion.

2. HUINENG

J. ENO; 638-713

ORIGINALLY THERE IS NOT A SINGLE THING

ONE DAY, sometime around the year 655, a young man working in the marketplace in the Chinese city of Nanhai heard words from the Diamond Sutra, one of the principal teachings of Buddhism, being recited by a traveler. Many years later the man wrote in what was described as his memoir, "On hearing these words, my mind cleared and I understood." The young man's name was Dajian Huineng (J. Daikan Eno), and he was to become the renowned sixth patriarch of Chinese Zen, whose teachings shaped Zen as we know it today.

Huineng was an unlikely candidate for such a position. His father died when he was young, and at the time of his meeting with the sutra-reciting traveler he was living in poverty, supporting himself and his mother on proceeds from selling firewood. In addition, he was not only poor, he was illiterate. And yet "his mind cleared and he understood" when he heard those words from the Diamond Sutra.

Huineng's understanding was not the same as rational understanding. It was not an understanding that comes from the limited human mind—from knowledge—but an understanding that emanates from what Zen calls "not-mind" or, as Bodhidharma expressed it, "no-knowing" mind. This understanding is an intuitive sensing through which all who undertake the practice of Zen awaken to their truth—a sensing that can be vague and fleeting but that must be caught before it is again covered up by the mind's limited knowledge. This "understanding beyond understanding" is the opening into a realization of the *essential reality* of this moment, unencumbered by conditioned ideas or concepts produced by the ego-mind; it is the opening into a mind that functions freely in everyday life—a primary teaching of the Diamond Sutra.

The point here is that it was Huineng's illiteracy that allowed him to understand. He was born at the dawn of the great Tang Dynasty, China's Golden Age of learning, arts, craftsmanship, and power, when education was seen as a sign of great wisdom. But his lack of education, his illiteracy, saved him from the burdens of an educated mind. His lack of the kind of knowledge that was so prized in the seventh century, as it is today, allowed him to understand without first having to metaphorically "burn the scriptures," as so many other educated, pre-enlightened Zen teachers first had to do—and as we have to do. The teaching here is clear: enlightenment, or awakening, is not about knowledge. Yet how much trust do we have in *that?* Do we ever see our lack of knowledge not as a failing but as a gift? Our mind, of course, holds "information" to be paramount, necessary, safe. If I can understand something, I am safe. If I can prove it, I am safe. So our mind has a difficult time allowing us to metaphorically burn our knowledge. But it is what we must do. All knowledge, Zen teaches, is an illusion, just as power, wealth, possessions, and self-image are.

HUINENG'S PERSONAL STORY and his teachings are compiled in what is known as the Platform Sutra, though modern scholarship has pretty much determined that this sutra was written by a disciple after the master's death. But this really has no effect on the power of the work itself. Yes, Huineng's life is described in embellished terms, but it is a story that must be told as is, for it has much to teach us. There is also Japanese Master Keizan's version of the sixth patriarch's life in the *Transmission of Light*, written in the thirteenth century, which shares an insight that offers wonderful inspiration for our practice. Keizan tells us that after his awakening, a small group of people invited Huineng to be part of their temple, sensing his deep wisdom. But after a while, Huineng thought to himself, "I seek the great teaching. Why should I stop halfway?"

"I seek the great teaching. Why should I stop halfway?" What encouraging words, tucked away in the *Transmission of Light*. Why should I stop halfway—and not practice with more depth? Not plunge more deeply into the frustration of not-knowing? Not endure the discomforts and disciplines of Zen practice? Not sit fully rather than coast? Not find a teacher? Not be fully mindful in doing my daily tasks? Why should I stop halfway and not devote myself wholeheartedly to the Way? I seek the great teaching. Why on earth should I stop halfway? Huineng certainly did not. He set out to find a teacher.

The teaching of Bodhidharma, who had died more than one hundred years before, had by now begun to permeate Buddhist sensibility in China, and his subtle insight of "not-mind, not-knowing," passed on through his disciples Huike and Seng Fu, was slowly taking root. This new "way" called itself simply "meditation"—Chan (or *Zen* as it would be called later in Japanese). Its leading proponent in the middle of the seventh century was Master Daman Hongren (J. Daiman Konin), who appears to have led a community of monks on East Mountain on Twin Peaks in Hubei Province, and whose students were slowly spreading the way of meditation throughout the land. He was later named the fifth patriarch and, as Andy Ferguson points out in his book *Zen's Chinese Heritage*, "Hongren's influence on Zen's historical development is difficult to overstate." It was to this teacher and to this new way that Huineng was drawn.

So it was that after what must have been an arduous journey, this poor, insignificant, illiterate, twenty-four-year-old man of lowly birth found himself before Master Hongren himself. Here is their exchange in an abridged version:

> "Where are you from? What are you looking for?"
> "I come from the south. I wish to be a buddha."
> "If you come from the south, you must be a barbarian. How can *you* be a buddha?"
> "People may be southerners or northerners, but in buddha nature there can be no south or north. I may be a barbarian but what difference is there in our buddha nature?"

"What difference is there in our buddha nature?" Indeed, what difference? It is a question to ask ourselves of all whom we meet. What difference is there in our common essentialness?

On hearing Huineng's reply, Master Hongren must have known he had someone highly gifted in front of him, but what did he do? In his wisdom he kept Huineng exactly as he was: a laborer, illiterate, unremarkable, even despised. He sent Huineng to work in the rice mill to see if he would be satisfied with the "just this" of that labor or if he desired to be someone special—a monk in the Dharma hall. Huineng himself grasped the need to hold to the discipline and acceptance of the "just this," for, the story tells us, he didn't even dare walk outside the Dharma hall in case he was tempted to go inside. When the mind functions freely, without dwelling on anything, without desiring anything more, does it matter whether one is in the rice shed or the Dharma hall? Whether one is a laborer or a monk or an abbot? Striving not to be tempted by something more, learning how to be satisfied with what is given, was the practice offered to Huineng by his astute teacher.

So Huineng worked for eight months as a common laborer in the monastery's rice mill without ever speaking with the master, without ever entering the Dharma hall. Would we be able to accept such a lot? Do we accept the utter ordinariness, the hard work, the boredom, the nonspecialness of our metaphorical rice mills—the meditation mat, our ordinary life? Or do we seek *enlightenment*? Enlightenment is not a thing, not something other, not something special, not somewhere else. It is to be realized right here in this moment—this ordinary moment—not outside of it. Holding ourselves in this moment is the primary work of Zen practice, for it is the only place where true enlightenment happens. But oh, how long it takes for us to fully accept this. It seems Huineng learned to accept it as he toiled away in the rice mill.

During this time, events began to unfold. One day, quite unexpectedly, Hongren told the assembled monks that they spent too much time on unimportant rituals without realizing the true liberation of the Way. "You disciples make offerings all day long and seek only the field of blessings, but you do not seek to escape from the bitter sea of birth and death." He went on to give them a task. "All of you return to your rooms and look into yourselves. Men of wisdom will of themselves grasp the original nature of their *prajna* (wisdom) intuition. Each of you, write a verse and bring it to me. I will read your verses, and if there is one who is awakened to the cardinal meaning, I will give him the robe and the Dharma and make him the sixth patriarch. Hurry, hurry!"

The monks went off and discussed the matter between themselves, coming to the conclusion that they would never be able to write such a deep verse, because of their ignorance. So "they all then gave up trying and did not have the courage to present a verse." (Modern-day practitioners may be familiar with such giving up and lack of courage. It assails us all.) They deferred to the head monk, a man named Shenxiu, asking him to write the verse for them. Shenxiu, however, had a difficult time doing this and struggled for four days. Finally he fashioned his verse, but decided to write it anonymously on the outer wall of the Dharma hall, figuring that if accepted by the master he would claim it as his own, and if not he would step down as head monk and give up practice of the Way. He was hedging his bets, clearly unsure of his insight, full of doubt. He could not trust his insight and so he could not fully own it.

Surely we can empathize with such doubt. Do we, too, at times, not trust our insights, question them, discard them before making them known? Why? To save face? To avoid looking like a failure? To avoid taking risks? Zen is all about taking risks, for in Zen we constantly walk into the unknown. As we reflect on Shenxiu's timid, anonymous action, might it help us to see our own timidity whenever we hesitate to express our insights directly? Might such reflection offer us courage to speak?

After finishing his verse, Shenxiu walked to the Dharma hall and when nobody was looking wrote this on its wall:

The body is the Tree of Wisdom,
The mind but a bright mirror.
At all times diligently polish it,
To remain untainted by dust.

But after he wrote it, doubt about what he had written persisted. He could not sleep that night and lay awake, uneasy and caught up in thought. I am sure we can all empathize with such a night. We have all been there one way or another, haven't we? But notice two key words here: *thought* and *uneasy*. Discriminating thought brings doubt, discriminating thought brings unease. "No thought," a still mind, if we learn to trust it, brings liberation—and sleep!

The next day, the master saw the verse. He saw that it had right insight but not yet *full* insight. Wipe the mirror clean, never let dust settle on it. Yes, this is what we continually must strive to practice in Zen—to wipe away the dust of the countless delusions to which we attach ourselves— but it is not yet a grasp of essential nature itself. Master Hongren told Shenxiu (for he realized who had written the anonymous verse) that the verse was good but that he had not yet realized full understanding—he had only arrived outside the gate. "You must enter the gate and see your own original nature." Hongren told him to go and write another.

Nevertheless, the master instructed the other monks to learn the verse as an encouragement for their own practice of diligently polishing away the dust of their delusions, and, back at the rice shed, Huineng overheard one of the dutiful monks reciting it. "As soon as I heard it I knew that the person who had written it had yet to know his one nature and to discern the cardinal meaning." When Huineng found out that the verse was written on the wall of the Dharma hall, he asked to be taken there to have someone write his verse for him, for he could not write.

Huineng's verse appeared next to Shenxiu's and this is what it said:

> The Tree of Wisdom fundamentally does not exist.
> Nor is there a stand for the mirror.
> Originally, there is not a single thing,
> So where would dust alight?

Originally, fundamentally, not one thing exists, for a thing, any thing, is an idea created by the ego-mind to give the thing some meaning and set it apart. Try it for yourself. Still your mind (stop thinking) for a few seconds, then look at an object without naming it or thinking about it.

Does it exist? When the mind is still, no-thing exists. Every thing, then, is no-thing. Reality just *is*, nonseparated and complete. Where then can dust settle? What mirror is there to wipe and who is there to wipe it?

When Master Hongren read Huineng's verse, he saw the deep insight of the person who wrote it and knew at once who that person was. Huineng was called to the master's room in the darkness, so he would not be seen by potentially jealous monks, and Hongren proceeded to take him through the Diamond Sutra—the diamond that cuts through delusions. When it came to the part where it said, "you should develop a mind that functions freely, without depending on anything or any place," Huineng fully awakened. He realized that reality is one, that even though one's conditioned mind perceives reality as two, it is also not-two. The fullness of this realization comes, as it did for Huineng, when all vestiges of duality drop off: no subject, no object, no me, no you, nothing outside of me, no me apart from anything. Reality in its multiple differences is empty of any differences—the supreme teaching of the Diamond Sutra—realized when the mind, creator of differences, is still. Huineng had fully awakened to the essence of reality, and the transmission of the Dharma was complete. Of course, nothing had been transmitted, for in Oneness there is nothing to transmit.

Following his realization, Huineng received the outward symbols of teaching authority—the traditional robe and bowl—in the middle of the night. (This, tradition holds, is why until recent times the Zen transmission ceremony for new teachers was held in private and during the night.) Master Hongren, however, understood his monks very well. Knowing what howls of envy would arise when they heard that the succession had gone to an illiterate young laborer who had never set foot in the Dharma hall, he realized that Huineng's very life was at stake. Acting wisely, Master Hongren told his new Dharma successor that he would have to go into hiding in the south of China until the appropriate time to teach arrived, and he escorted Huineng to the riverboat station. Upon securing a boat, the master offered to row Huineng across but Huineng replied that a person who had realized the truth no longer needed assistance. "When one is enlightened, one ferries oneself over."

One can imagine tears of gratitude arising in Master Hongren's eyes on hearing Huineng's words. He gave his farewell and turned to go back to the monastery. Once there, for a day or so, he gave no talks. When questioned about this he said, "The Dharma has gone to the south." At this, the monks perked up their ears and asked the master who had received the teaching. The master replied: "The capable one got it." Now, in Chinese, the word *neng* means capable, so immediately the monks knew that it was Huineng. The howl went up, as predicted: total incomprehension, envy. The unfairness! The injustice of this! Here they'd been practicing diligently, enduring the rigors of Zen for years, and this illiterate, foreign laborer had received the transmission after only eight months.

This cry of injustice, leading to anger and revenge, surely resonates with us all. But Zen teaches us that life is neither fair nor unfair. Life just is. Fair and unfair are both creations of the ignorant ego-mind—another reason to practice stilling this mind. For when it is still, we can more easily accept the "just this" of a situation and respond to it in the appropriate manner. Accepting the "just this" of a situation does not mean we lose our authority or become carpets for others to walk on. It simply means that we receive the situation as it is and respond accordingly, but with an egoless mind. The action of an egoless mind, whether active or passive, is always right action.

A band of the most outraged monks set out after Huineng to reclaim the robe and bowl that they thought rightfully belonged to one of their own. The band was led by a man named Huiming. Before becoming a monk, Huiming had been a four-star general in the Chinese army; he was tough and he knew how to wield authority. He ran ahead of the others and caught up with Huineng on the road to the south, near Mount Dayu. When Huineng saw from afar that someone was running after him, he didn't flee or hide. He stopped and waited. And when the monk-general caught up with him, Huineng took the robe and bowl out of his knapsack and put them on a rock. Huiming went to take them but, as the story goes, he could not lift them. He began to tremble. It was his first moment of awakening. The Dharma cannot be taken by force. It can only be surrendered to.

"Workman!" he called out. "Workman! I have come for the teaching, not for the robe! Teach me!" What a moment. The crowd mentality of "this robe is ours, this bowl is mine, my right, my possession" dropped off, and the authentic seeker in Huiming was revealed. The authoritarian general gave way to the receiving monk. The need to possess, the need to control, the greed and desire that, as the Buddha taught, only lead to suffering, dropped off and Huiming was a beginner again. Teach me! Teach me! For us, it is the moment when our ego is stripped away, the moment our self-image, our specialness, our titles, and our knowledge all drop off and we realize that we too are beginners. The minute we think there is nothing else for us to learn, we are headed in the wrong direction.

Huineng then said to his first student, "When your mind does not create good, does not create bad, what is your original face?" When your mind is still, Huineng is asking—when you are not caught up in mine, yours, right, wrong, fair, unfair, success, failure—who are you? Is there a "you?" What is your original face? What is your true self? The general had practiced, and practiced strongly, up to this moment. So when this moment came, all he needed was the right question—"the turning word" as they say in Zen—to help him break through: "What is your original face?" This question, of course, cannot be answered by the ego-mind. Ego-mind must be stilled for us to realize our original face. This is why we practice, and practice is what the general had done in the monastery. Now he got it. He broke out in a sweat and bowed in gratitude. His original, true self was manifested, for he had genuinely realized that his identity did not lie in titles or possessions or robes or rituals—did not lie in being right or wrong but in just being.

After most moments of enlightenment, doubt is usually just around the corner, and this moment was no exception. In the middle of his deep bow of gratitude, Huiming stopped and said, "Teacher, besides these secret words and secret meanings you have just unfolded for me, is there anything deeper? Is there anything *more*?" How very human. Haven't we all been there? "It can't be that simple," we say, "there's got to be something more that I'm missing." Trust and confidence in our insight begins to evaporate as doubt comes rolling in. Huineng heard the doubt and he met it. "I have not revealed anything that is a secret. If you reflect on your original face—in other words, if you go beyond your self-created identity and reflect on who you *really* are—you will find that the secret is in *you*."

Huiming heard Huineng's response and said to him, "All these years with Master Hongren and the other monks, I never realized my true self [though, one could point out, he was practicing]. Now, thanks to you, I am like a man who drinks water and knows for himself whether it is warm or cold. Be my teacher." And the new master replied, "Master Hongren is teacher to us both." So Huiming took his leave and returned to the monastery. He told the others, "I have climbed the heights but could not find him." Indeed. He had found himself instead.

LATER ON, Huiming became abbot of a monastery and changed his name to Daoming so as not to have a name similar to that of Huineng. And what happened to the other characters? Master Hongren continued teaching in the monastery until his death in 675, and Shenxiu, the head monk, had a full life. He went back to the Dharma hall after being told his realization had not yet fully flowered. There he practiced diligently, and eventually broke through the gateless gate. He became Master Hongren's second Dharma successor and went on to hold the esteemed position in northern China known as the northern patriarch. The future southern patriarch, Huineng, continued south and went into hiding for fifteen years. Why, we do not know. Perhaps he was honing his insight, allowing the Dharma to ripen until he knew for himself that he was ready. He took refuge with a group of hunters in the mountains and, in the Platform Sutra, tells an endearing little story about himself. Apparently the hunters had him take care of the nets that caught animals they were going to eat. Huineng wrote, "Whenever they were not looking, I let the animals go. When I was asked about this, I simply put more vegetables in the pot." How human these ancestors of ours were!

So Huineng lived an anonymous life for fifteen years, seemingly content to live in the here and now of "just this." We, in our hectic, impatient lives, need to pay attention to such an example. We need to become aware of how unwilling we so often are to just remain where we are, doing one thing for as long as we need to do it. We seem to be always multitasking, always trying to get ahead, to be somewhere else, not satisfied with having to put in the hidden time necessary to truly awaken. If we are not where we want to be because of comparisons with others or because of an idea of where we think we should be, we must keep surrendering to where we are, always coming back to right here, right now, just this. Practicing this way, we will eventually realize that where we are is the perfect place to be, no matter how incomplete, muddled, or messy it may seem.

After fifteen years, Huineng left the mountains and found his way to a monastery in Guang Province where the venerable Yintsung was delivering lectures on the Nirvana Sutra. Standing in the monastery courtyard, presumably on a break between the lectures, Huineng heard two monks having an argument about the flag flying above the Dharma hall, a story that comes to us as koan 29 in *The Gateless Gate*. One monk said, "The flag moves," while the other said, "The wind moves." This argument continued until Huineng walked over to them and said, "It is not the wind that moves, it is not the flag that moves. It is your mind that moves." The two monks were struck with awe.

We must consider that these were two monks in training. They surely knew conceptually, as we may know conceptually, that everything is essentially One—that there is only one mind. Perhaps the analogy of waves and ocean may help here: there is only one ocean, and there are many waves. Each wave is the ocean. Each wave is not separate from the ocean. So when the wave moves it is really the ocean that moves. There is no wave outside of the ocean, just as there is no flag and no wind outside of mind. So it is not the flag that moves and not the wind that moves, it is mind that moves. Yet the two monks had gotten tied up in the dualism created by their limited, conditioned ego-minds, a dualism that is the cause of all suffering, as the Buddha taught. They had been arguing, wasting energy on "is it this or is it that?" It is always wasted energy when we spend time on "is it this or is it that?" and when we compare and judge what is right or wrong, good or bad, better or worse.

Rice shed, abbot's seat—ultimately there isn't any difference. This is why, in reality, we cannot suffer because suffering is another creation of the ego-mind. This insight into nonsuffering is where this magnificent flag teaching takes us. Huineng does not interfere in the discussion to show that he's smarter than the monks. Rather, out of his compassionate awareness, he sees that they are suffering—for are they not arguing? Is not argument always about opposition, and is not opposition based on dualism? These two monks—who, of course, are us—see the flag and the wind as outside of themselves, and they see each other as outside of themselves, as well. Seeing the other as outside of oneself is the basis of all argument, enmity, hatred, war, and killing. Realizing this teaching, even being willing to undertake exploring this seemingly absurd proposition that it is the mind that moves and not the wind or the flag, has profound implications for us as we live in relationships and in community. It seems to me that it is the authentic basis of nonviolence, for blaming the other is never the way to grow. The problem does not rest with the other; the problem rests with oneself because the idea of anything being a problem is a creation of one's limited ego-mind.

Word of Huineng's statement about the waving flag reached the venerable Yintsung, and Huineng's true identity as successor to Master Hongren was revealed. Eventually Huineng became abbot of Baolin Monastery near Shaozhou (baolin means "precious woods"), where he taught for the next thirty years, gaining renown as the Buddhist teacher who emphasized meditation as the way to enlightenment outside of scriptures. Chan/Zen was now beginning to forge its own voice within the other Buddhist schools, and Huineng's insight and teaching, compiled in the Platform Sutra, was its foundation. This is why he is so deeply honored by all Zen lines as "the great sixth patriarch" and why the Platform Sutra is given the title of sutra, the only Buddhist text that is not a direct teaching of the Buddha to receive such an honor.

According to tradition, Huineng had twenty-six successors, two of whom were the forebears of all successive Zen teachers. His recorded teachings in the Platform Sutra continue to guide us to this day. Let us leave the sixth patriarch as he gives his last talk before his death:

Today I say goodbye to you. After I die, don't mourn me in the usual manner of the world. If you receive other people's condolences, offerings, and observances, or if you wear mourning clothes, then this is not the true school, and you are not my disciples. You should act as though I were still in the world, sitting completely upright, not moving, not resting, without creation or passing away, not going or coming, without positive or negative, but just in solitary peace. This is the Great Way. After I die, just go on practicing as before, as though I were still here. If you go against this teaching, it is as though my life here as abbot were meaningless.

And so Huineng died. The year was 713. He was seventy-five years old. Today, because of him, we can each say to ourselves: "I seek the great teaching. Why should I stop halfway?"

3. MAZU

ORDINARY MIND IS THE WAY

OF HUINENG'S twenty-six Dharma successors, two were to become teachers of students whose lives and teachings defined Zen further and moved it forward into what is generally regarded as its Golden Age. These two "grandsons in the Dharma" of Huineng were Mazu Daoyi (J. Baso Doitsu) and Shitou Xiqian (J. Sekito Kisen), whose descendants formed not only the Linji (J. Rinzai) and Dongshan (J. Tozan) schools of Zen—both of which exist to this day—but also three other schools of Zen which subsequently died out. Japanese, Korean, and now Western Zen all owe their roots to the insights and teachings of these two giants, who lived at approximately the same time and were widely regarded as the two leading Zen masters in China. It was said that you were not a complete practitioner unless you had studied with them both. They never met but respected each other's teaching.

Mazu's family name was Ma, but after he was given the honorific *su* (great master), he became known as Mazu. Of all the Chinese teachers, he is the only one who kept his family name; all other teachers took the name of the district in which their monastic centers were located. Mazu was born in 709, and his life spanned most of the eighth century—the arising years of that Golden Age of Zen. He came from far western China, near Tibet, and apparently his father was a garbage collector. He left home at the age of fifteen and, historical texts tell us, "From the time of his youth, he despised the dust of the earth, renounced all clinging and dependency, and yearned for the freedom of the itinerant life." What an apt description of the way of Zen—no clinging, moving with the constant change of each moment, adapting, flowing with the stream. It would seem that even as a very young man, Mazu was primed for such a way of living.

After becoming a monk in his early years, Ma studied with several Buddhist teachers but finally, in his early forties, chose to remain with the first Dharma successor of Master Huineng, the Zen master Nanyue Huairang (J. Nangaku Ejo), with whom he studied for ten years on Mount Heng before becoming his Dharma heir. *The Record of Mazu* tells us that Ma was a devoted student. He practiced meditation relentlessly, something that eventually caught the master's eye. One day, outside the hermitage, Nanyue approached Ma and asked him a really important question: "I see you are sitting in meditation a great deal, monk. Why?" Ma answered, "I wish to become a buddha." Nanyue picked up a tile and began to rub it with a stone. Ma watched him and then after a while asked, "What are you doing, master?" "I'm polishing this tile in order to make it a mirror." "How can you make a mirror by polishing a tile?" Ma asked incredulously. "How can you make a buddha by practicing meditation?" said Nanyue. Ma was thunderstruck and his mind cleared. He awoke to the truth of who he really was—already a buddha.

Nanyue had been the first Dharma heir of Huineng, and in this exchange we can see how, through very skillful means, he reflects his teacher's deep insight, as well as his own. Remember that in his verse transcribed for him on the wall of the Dharma hall, Huineng expressed the uselessness of polishing to make oneself better. A generation later, Nanyue demonstrated this wordlessly with his tile. What were they both teaching? To break open your ego-mind's associations, which say, "If I polish, I get something; if I sit hard enough, I become someone else." This becoming something else is the world of gain, the world of two, the world of discrimination in which one sees oneself—and buddha or awakened nature—as two separate realities. We already *are* buddha and awakened nature. How can we become something we already are?

So keep polishing, but not to make a mirror. Stop seeking to be awakened, to be enlightened, to be better through meditation: just meditate, just do zazen. Stop polishing that tile for the wrong reason. Stop meditating for the wrong reason. Just polish! Just sit! For the amazing news is that when you are just a polisher, just a sitter, you *are* a buddha—the buddha you sought to become through polishing or meditating. This is what a buddha is, this is what being awakened is—to just be a polisher, a sitter, a walker, an eater, a worker, a sleeper, without any intention of gain. Just this. And how do you become a polisher and a sitter whose true intent is just to polish or to sit? During these activities you still the restless ego-mind that is the creator of dualism, creator of discrimination and judgment, creator of the notion of results, and which tells you, "You must make something else or become someone else. You must *become* a buddha." Still the restless ego-mind and you will realize that a buddha is not something else, and it is not someone else. Stop meditating to become someone else. Just meditate, just sit.

Did Ma stop sitting after his teacher showed him that he could not become a buddha through sitting? Of course not. His teacher's skillful means having penetrated his ignorance, he realized the uselessness of his efforts to become something he already was, and he stopped seeking to become awakened. He just sat, practicing awareness in this moment, then the next, then the next, and so forth, for to stop such practice is to slip immediately into the dualistic mindset. He practiced with his teacher for about ten years, after which he received Nanyue's seal of transmission and became his Dharma successor at the age of fifty-two in the year 761.

HERE WE NEED to become familiar with events in China that are hardly ever mentioned in Zen teaching, but which affected both Mazu and Shitou, since they both taught during the same time. Roshi Joan Sutherland writes that these were turbulent years. Chinese culture and power, which had been flourishing for two hundred years under the Tang dynasty, was beginning to show signs of strain. The country was large; it had many borders to defend from ever-more-powerful bordering states. And because it needed money for these military operations, the populace was heavily taxed. Farmers were forced to become soldiers to defend the borders, and so less and less food was grown. Riots developed and the government had to call in foreign mercenaries to quell them. One of these mercenaries, a Turkish general named An Lushan, gained favor at court with the emperor's favorite courtesan and by 755 had amassed so much power that he rose and declared himself emperor, setting up a rebel stronghold and almost bringing down the Tang dynasty, which never fully recovered. More significantly, this ushered in, as Sutherland writes, "ten years of civil war, famine, disease so devastating that two out of three Chinese died. *Two out of three.*" In 764, the national census counted seventeen million Chinese, down from fifty-three million ten years earlier. In the space of less than ten years, China went from being a mighty empire to a nation in ruins. Luku, the great Chinese poet, wrote at the time:

> The nation is destroyed
> Mountains and rivers remain.

Such devastation must have had an immense impact on Mazu, for it was during the An Lushan rebellion that Mazu was studying with Nanyue, received transmission, and began what was to be twenty years of travel throughout China. Little is recorded of where he traveled but what is certain is that his insights were born in a hard and cruel environment that included unimaginable famine and violence. Think, perhaps, of the modern-day genocide in Rwanda. How could this not affect Mazu's teaching? How could it not affect Shitou's teaching? How could it not affect Zen? How could Mazu and Shitou remain in a meditative ivory tower in the midst of such devastation? They were forced to look at the devastation and find buddha nature there. Both Mazu and Shitou lived through hard times, and it was out of such hard times that Zen blossomed.

Whatever setbacks or crises we have in our own lives today probably pale in comparison with the afflictions suffered by those who came to Mazu's monastery during China's devastation. But a question for our own reflection might be whether our own practice and insight blossoms during hard times. Does our practice deepen during times of crisis, times of setbacks or unexpected roadblocks? Do we use such hard times skillfully by facing them, not getting derailed by them, by learning from them, finding teaching in them, growing from them? Or do we blame the hard times for our hard times? If only things were different; if only that hadn't happened; if only he, she, they were not what they are; it is all *their* fault. "If only": the cause of withdrawal, separation, and endless longing. This is little more than self-pity and lost focus, stagnation rather than growth.

It seems to me that we awaken more profoundly out of hard times than out of the calm times in our life. It is telling that the Chinese symbol for crisis is the same as that for opportunity. Crisis and opportunity are indeed one and the same. When we are faced with a setback or difficulty, we as Zen practitioners always have the opportunity to either label whatever is happening "difficult," "failure," or "crisis"—or not to label it at all and instead see it as "just this." This view of reality, without labels, allows for all kinds of possibilities to arise if we could only trust the moment. Developing such trust is the work of Zen. It will depend on the strength of our practice and our ability to be aware when we are creating a label. If we are not aware, we will get, as Pema Chodron puts it, "hooked by the bait" created by our ego-mind. But once we can see the labeling we are doing, it is much easier to detach from the labels and allow the moment to reveal its possibilities. As the Dhammapada puts it: "It is good to tame and monitor the mind which is flighty and difficult to restrain, rushing wherever it will, subtle, difficult to perceive, and restless. A mind well monitored, a tamed mind, brings happiness." Taming and monitoring the ego-mind is our primary Zen work in a crisis because a tamed mind sees the opportunities in hard times and seizes them.

For twenty years Mazu traveled all over China, finally settling down at the age of seventy-two in Zhongling in southern China where he taught for the next ten years before his death. During that time he nurtured either 80 or 139 or Dharma successors, depending on the source—more than any Zen teacher in history—and he pioneered new methods of teaching, described below, that we still follow in Zen today.

Those who came to Mazu's monastery did not receive comfort and solace. As Sutherland writes, "Anyone looking for escape at Ma's monastery was in for a shock." And anyone looking for escape in Zen today is in for a shock. Zen is not about fleeing reality but about *meeting* reality, and meeting and accepting reality can be awesomely difficult. That is why so many people give up. Illusion can be so much easier to bear. What of the novice monk coming to Mazu's monastery? Did he find genuine freedom in clinging to the illusion of his ancestral home, now devastated? Did he find freedom in clinging to the sorrow, to the bitter thoughts, to the anger over the death of his parents and siblings from famine? Did he find freedom in clinging to the illusion of being able to escape from life's hell into a serene interior life within the monastery walls? He did not, for he was not given the opportunity to do so. In Mazu's monastery there was none of the introspection and formal lecturing that had defined Zen teaching and practice up to now. A novice monk was now met with a new method of teaching.

Mazu's new method drew on "the immediacy of insight" realized by his grandfather in the Dharma, Master Huineng. Recall that the illiterate Huineng did not need sutras and rituals to awaken. He realized the truth in the immediacy of the moment. Two generations later, Mazu's teaching approach to this was to depend not solely on lectures but also to meet with students on a one-on-one, face-to-face basis— the predecessor of *dokusan*, or *daisan*, as it is called in Zen today. In such one-on-one meetings, the student's mind was immediately cut off, before it could begin spinning off into delusion, through a method of "kicks and shouts" for which Mazu became famous. Here are three short exchanges, paraphrased from *The Record of Mazu*, that demonstrate this teaching in action:

Someone asked, "What is the meaning of Zen?" The master hit him and said, "If I didn't hit you, people everywhere would laugh at me."

Someone asked, "What is the meaning of Zen?" The master replied, "What is the meaning of now?"

Venerable Shuilo came to see the master for the first time. He asked, "What is the meaning of Zen?" The master said, "Bow down." As he bowed down, the master kicked him in the chest. Shuilo had great awakening. He rose, laughing. Later he told the assembly, "Since the day I was kicked by Master Ma, I have not stopped laughing."

This method of kicks and shouts, which was later finely honed by Mazu's Dharma heirs Huangbo and Linji, can feel repugnant to us. However, on reflection, one can see why the master used it with traumatized people. It was like throwing cold water onto them. Wake up! Mazu did not hit or shout to punish, but to awaken. Essentially it was compassionate teaching meant to knock out thinking. "Don't ask illusory questions," he was saying with each shout or blow. "Be with NOW/THIS [shout/blow] because NOW/THIS is the only reality. Wake up from your thoughts of your village, you monk, your thoughts of home, of family, of have and have not! These are dreams and are not real. This kick is real! This shout is real! Be awake—now! Be alive—now! Experience the kick, experience the shout. Experience it! Let it shock you into life!"

The Transmission of the Lamp tells us that Mazu's personality was a rough one—he had the stride of a bull and the penetrating eyes of a tiger. Surely such an appearance, coupled with his shouts and blows, must have been difficult to take, especially for those seeking solace in his presence. And yet flocks of people came to study with him, and he had, as mentioned above, more Dharma successors than any other teacher in Zen history. Zen seeks to develop urgency and immediacy in all who undertake its practice because we too, like those monks, constantly live in dreams from which we need to awaken. All the tools and disciplines of Zen practice are meant to cut off the mind's delusions, which are the cause of all dissatisfaction and suffering. Ours is an endless practice because, as we know, our delusions are endless and they keep us from realizing who we really are.

MAZU'S TEACHING WAS FOUNDED on what is known as the *tathagatagarbha* doctrine, based on the teaching of ancient sutras such as the Lankavatara Sutra and the Avatamsaka Sutra. Tsungmi, a Zen master living around the time of Mazu, wrote this about the *tathagatagarbha* doctrine:

> This teaching says that all sentient beings possess the true mind of emptiness and quiescence whose nature is without inception, fundamentally pure. Bright, unobscured, astute, and constantly aware... It is called Buddha-nature; it is also called *tathagatagarbha* and mind-ground. From time without beginning it has been concealed by false thoughts.

This "mind-ground" functions not *in* the world but *as* the world, and it is this functioning of "mind-ground" that is the basis of Mazu's teaching. Essential nature is not a thing, Mazu is saying. It has no signs of its own and it cannot be thought or imagined. But it functions or manifests in the reality of the world. It acts and its actions are nothing other than *our* actions in everyday life. Mazu called this functioning "ordinary mind" and famously taught that "ordinary mind is the Way." This was another huge step in the evolution of Zen. "Not one thing exists," taught Huineng; yet it functions, taught Mazu.

This is why Mazu, and all Zen teaching, is so adamant about always bringing us back to reality. Mazu's kicks and shouts are simply dramatic ways of saying that "just this," "just here," and "just now" are the only places where we can act and in turn awaken to the truth of reality, which can be realized at any given moment of our life and is always available to us. What keeps us separated from this truth is the ego-mind's conditioned misinformation. We call this ignorance, one of the three poisons in Zen Buddhism (the other two being greed and hatred)—ignorance about the truth of who we really are. We are all one, true mind. We are not separate from true mind; we *are* true mind—or Buddha, God, Yahweh, Allah, or whatever poor name we choose to give to the unnamable, the unknowable, the unimaginable. We are not separate from this mind-ground as Zen calls it, no matter what is happening. So if I am angry or greedy or put others down, I am not separate from true mind. If I worry, have doubts, fail, or feel I am not good enough, I am not separate from true mind. If I lie or steal, I am not separate from true mind. Isn't that amazing? It is so amazing that we can't even allow ourselves to *think* it might be true—that a greedy, angry, anxiety-ridden, never-good-enough person is in this very moment a buddha.

Yet there is a big difference between an ignorant person and a buddha or awakened person. The greedy, angry, anxiety-ridden, not-good-enough person—the ignorant person—does not realize that he or she *is* buddha, but the awakened person does, clearly seeing that the endlessly arising human seeds of greed, anger, and hatred are illusions created by the grasping ego-mind. It is this realization that allows the awakened person to resist getting caught by these illusory baits and to transcend them. Greed, anger, hatred, and ignorance will always be there because they are part of our humanity, but an enlightened person realizes their illusory nature and resists getting trapped by them. This is ignorance versus enlightenment. Ignorance and enlightenment are not about how much one does or does not know. They are about realizing who one truly is—in this moment. This moment is not separate from who one truly is, and that is the heart of Mazu's compassionate teaching of the kick or the shout. You are not separate from true mind, he is telling us; you can never *be* separate. Your doubt is not separate from true mind, your searching question is not separate from true mind, your greed, anger, and ignorance are not separate from true mind. See this! Shout! Kick! Now! Here! And wake up to who you really are!

In the eighth century, stilling the ignorant mind was called "cultivation of true mind." True mind can't be cultivated, but its realization can and must be cultivated. As Mazu himself said, "If one says there is no need for cultivation then that is the same as ordinary [ignorant] people." In other words, we need to practice in order to see that we don't *need* to practice. In saying this, Mazu surely must have remembered his awakening outside Nanyue's hermitage and his own subsequent cultivation.

Teaching that true mind is none other than ordinary mind was Mazu's central teaching. The word *ordinary* comes from the root *order*, and order is about "just one thing at a time." Ordinary mind is, therefore, attention to one thing at a time, one moment at a time—"just this." Grasp this and you grasp everything Mazu teaches. Grasp this and your practice (and your life) will be effortless as it moves with full attention from moment to moment to moment. Out of Mazu's teaching that true mind is not separate from ordinary mind, that they are "not-two," an awakened Zen life is lived.

Koan 73 of *The Blue Cliff Record*, freely adapted here, beautifully illus-
trates ordinary mind. A monk comes to Mazu and asks, "What is the
meaning of the way of Zen?" Mazu says, "Oh, today I'm tired, I cannot tell you about it. Go ask Xitang [his second Dharma heir]." So the
monk does, and Xitang says, "Oh, today I have a headache, I cannot
tell you about it. Go ask Baizhang [Mazu's first Dharma heir]." So the
monk does, and Baizhang says, "Hmmm...coming to this point, I do
not understand." The monk is perplexed and relays these encounters
to Mazu. Mazu says, "Xitang's head is white, Baizhang's head is black."
The way of Zen is "what is." Or, as the formidable thirteenth-century
Japanese master Dogen said when he returned to Japan after deepening
his Zen insight in China, "I have returned from my study in China realizing that my eyes are horizontal and my nose is vertical."

What is the meaning of the way of Zen? Obvious, ordinary life right
in front of us. "I'm tired" is true mind functioning; "I have a headache" is true mind functioning; "I'm really irritable today" is true mind
functioning; "I feel wonderful today" is true mind functioning; "I don't
understand" is true mind functioning. See this, realize this, and all
ideas of understanding or not understanding—all questions—drop off.
What's to know? What's to understand? What's to find if true mind and
I are not separate, not two?

IN THE YEAR 788, Mazu became ill. The head monk came and asked,
"How has the master's honored condition been lately?" Mazu said,
"Sun-face buddha, moon-face buddha." Sun-face buddha was said to
live for eighteen hundred years (forever); moon-face buddha was said to
live only one day and one night (not forever). Sun-face buddha, moon-
face buddha. Two and not-two. Then, on the first day of the second
lunar month, Mazu died. His body passed away but his teaching lives
and affects all who practice Zen to this day.

Mazu's body died but his essential nature lives—and it is us.

4. SHITOU

J. SEKITO; 700-790

A SAGE HAS NO SELF, YET THERE IS
NOTHING THAT IS NOT HIMSELF

I've built a grass hut where there's nothing of value.
After eating, I relax and enjoy a nap.
When it was completed, fresh weeds appeared.
Now it's been lived in—covered by weeds.

IN A GRASS HUT, high in the mountains of China, lived a true Zen hermit. Although most of the masters described in this book spent time in solitude, this seems to have been with an eye toward eventually teaching in more communal settings. This master in the grass hut chose to spend the better part of his life far from the activity of the world, not concerned with having to preach the Dharma, just totally committed to living it. Yet this hermit helped shape Zen Buddhism to such a degree that practitioners still follow his Dharma in the world today. Who was this man whose solitary life feels so different from our hectic modern ones?

His name was Shitou Xiqian (J. Sekito Kisen), and he was, like Mazu, a Dharma grandson of Zen Master Huineng, the towering sixth ancestor who formulated what became known as Chan, or Zen. Shitou's life, like Mazu's, covered practically the whole of the eighth century, and the two men spawned Dharma successors who were the ancestors of all subsequent Zen lineages throughout the world, their teaching based on the fundamental truth of the Oneness of all that is. Such Oneness is revealed when the discriminating, separating mind is stilled, and stilling that discriminating mind (also known in Zen as *ignorant mind*) is the fundamental work of Zen. Both Mazu and Shitou sought to still their students' discriminating minds but in different ways, as we shall see.

Shitou was born in 700, and his birthplace is given as Gaoyao in Duanzhou, not far from Baolin Monastery, the residence of Master Huineng himself. Tradition tells us that when Shitou was fourteen he met the great master just before Huineng's death, and the master told him to study with one of his Dharma heirs, Qingyuan Xingsi (J. Seigen Gyoshi). As with so many of these seminal teachers, it seems that Shitou was attracted to Chan at an early age, though it is interesting to note that according to the early biographies he did not receive ordination as a monk in the monastery at Lofushan until he was twenty-eight—a relatively mature age. Why did he not receive ordination earlier? We will probably never know, though his lack of haste does support the early record, which says that Shitou was endowed with "keen intelligence and quiet self-confidence." Perhaps he just wanted to take his time. Is there teaching here for us in our extraordinarily busy world? What's the rush?

Shortly after ordination, Shitou, like Mazu, was drawn to the newly emerging way of Chan and did indeed seek out Zen Master Qingyuan. He stayed with him for fourteen years, receiving Dharma transmission at the age of forty-two, though little is known of this period. Then, according to tradition, Shitou moved to the mountainous area of Hunan Province, an area that was at the time quite a spiritual hub, being the home of three Buddhist monasteries, as well as a Taoist and a Confucian center. Here he built himself a small hut on a large flat rock, and so he became known as Shitou, which means "Stone Head" or "Above the Rock." Shitou had essentially chosen the life of a hermit. After a time, however, his presence became known to local spiritual seekers and some began to visit him, asking for his teaching. And this is how he lived—meditating in his small hut and speaking with those who came to visit him, one-on-one. In this he was not much different from the hermits who still live in the mountains of China, and whose lives have been so beautifully documented by Edward A. Burger in his film *Amongst White Clouds* and by Steven R. Johnson in his photographs in *Where the World Does Not Follow.*

Shitou is said to have realized deep awakening on reading the words of the fourth-century sage Sengzhao, as described in the commentary on koan 91 in *The Book of Serenity,* though when this awakening occurred is not clear. Sengzhao had written, "The ultimate man is empty and hollow; he has no form, yet of the myriad things there is none that is not his own making. Who can understand the myriad things as oneself? Only a sage." To which Shitou added, "A sage has no self, yet there is nothing that is not himself." Out of this insight, he composed his great poem, "The Identity of Relative and Absolute or Harmony of Difference and Equality." Its title was borrowed from a Taoist text on the I Ching, and the work, known as the Sandokai in Japanese and chanted today in Soto monasteries and Zen centers, is honored in the Soto lineage by being the only teaching not taken directly from the Indian sutras (direct teachings of the Buddha) to be included in the Zen service.

> The mind of the Great Sage of India is intimately
> Conveyed from west to east.
> Among human beings are wise ones and fools,
> But in the Way there is no northern or southern patriarch.
> The subtle source is clear and bright;
> The tributary streams flow through the darkness.
> To be attached to things is illusion;
> To encounter the absolute is not yet enlightenment.
> Each and all, the subjective and objective spheres are related,
> And at the same time, independent.
> Related, yet working differently, though each keeps its own place.
> Form makes the character and appearance different.
> Sounds distinguish comfort and discomfort.
> The dark makes all words one.
> The brightness distinguishes good and bad phrases.
> The four elements return to their nature as a child to its mother.
> Fire is hot, wind moves, water is wet, earth hard.

Eyes see, ears hear, nose smells, tongue tastes the salt and sour.
Each is independent of the other.
Cause and effect must return to the great reality.
The words high and low are used relatively.
Within light there is darkness,
But do not try to understand that darkness.
Within darkness there is light,
But do not look for that light.
Light and darkness are a pair,
Like the foot before and the foot behind, in walking.
Each thing has its own intrinsic value and is
Related to everything else in function and position.
Ordinary life fits the absolute as a box and its lid.
The absolute works together with the relative
Like two arrows meeting in midair.
Reading words, you should grasp the great reality.
Do not judge by any standards.
If you do not see the Way, you do not see it even as you walk
    on it.
When you walk the Way, it is not near, it is not far.
If you are deluded, you are mountains and rivers away from it.
I respectfully say to those who wish to be enlightened:
Do not waste your time by night or day.

This is indeed a poem about harmony, the harmony of me and other, human and divine, absolute and relative, difference and sameness. Shitou's insight is primarily that of the Middle Way, the foundational insight of Siddhartha Gautama, the Buddha, who realized that liberation is not to be found in the separation of this and that but in the "not-two" of this and that. This and that are indeed this and that but also "not this" and "not that." This and that, then, are in complete harmony, "like two arrows meeting in midair," as the poem puts it. Viewing the world from the perspective of this "not-two" or "not separate" is the basic work of Zen. And this means not clinging to either this or that, not clinging to either the worldly or the not worldly. Early on in the poem, Shitou expresses the central insight of this Dharma: "To be attached to things is illusion, to encounter the absolute is not yet enlightenment."

In other words, it is not relative, it is not absolute; it is not human, it is not divine; it is not this, it is not that. Well, we might ask, what is it, then? That is the ultimate Zen question. The opening lines of the Heart Sutra, the central teaching of Mahayana Buddhism, express the answer: "Form is *exactly* emptiness, emptiness *exactly* form," or we could say "human is *exactly* divine, divine *exactly* human; this is *exactly* that, that is *exactly* this." But this is only the conceptual answer, someone else's answer. The only way to discover experientially for oneself if this is true is through meditation, when the human mind, creator of "this" and "that," is stilled, and when "not-two" is realized, if even for only a few seconds. It is also discovered through the constant rebalancing of the seesawing human mind, which keeps veering between the extremes of relative reality and absolute reality—the relative being the end it veers to most of the time. Do not cling to this world, do not cling to the absolute, warns Shitou. Neither is it and both are it. Realizing this is enlightenment.

In "The Identity of Relative and Absolute," Shitou also uses the images of darkness and light, but not in the expected way to be viewed as opposites, but rather to be realized as harmonious. The absolute is not light, as we might think, but darkness, for it is unknowable and opaque. It is this unknowable darkness that is light. The relative, or worldly, is not darkness, as we might think, but light, for it is seen and knowable. This knowable light is darkness. Light and darkness are not separate but in harmony, "like the foot before and the foot behind, in walking." The poem's last two lines seamlessly present the paradox of the Way: If you wish to be enlightened, "do not waste your time by night or day." In other words, if you want to wake up, don't bother, for you are already awake and there is nothing to achieve; if you want to wake up, don't waste your time and redouble your effort. Neither is the Way, and both are the Way.

Shitou's "The Identity of Relative and Absolute" is the ultimate expression of reconciliation. However, lest we imagine the master living some kind of otherworldly, out-of-touch life in the mountains, it is important to remember that he wrote this poem of harmony during one of the most nonharmonious times in China's history. Great unrest had begun to ferment in the nation just around the time Shitou took up residence in his small hut in the mid-740s, unrest that resulted in the ten-year An Lushan rebellion (755–764), described in chapter 3, when two-thirds of the population died—a staggering number. Can you imagine two-thirds of the population of the United States dying within ten years? It almost defies imagination, and yet this is what happened in China. It must have impacted even that remote mountain area, for people fleeing from the devastation probably sought refuge and solace in its spiritual communities.

How would Shitou have answered their probable despair? With what must have been a startling response: "What meets the eye is the Way." Like Mazu, he urged those who came to speak with him, many of whom were probably confused, sorrowful, helpless, angry, vengeful, and fearful, to look at and not away from the reality around them, to be with this reality. For only by being with it could they see through into its essential emptiness, see into the essential emptiness of the ignorant mind's values and desires and so be liberated from the prison of such desires. Here Shitou was one with the central teaching of the Buddha, expressed in the Four Noble Truths. The reality of life is never what our ignorant mind thinks it should be; ignorant mind's wanting the reality of life always to be something else is the actual suffering, not the reality itself; accepting reality as it is without wanting it to be something else is liberation from suffering. Look at reality as it is, with a still mind that is free of a desire for this or that outcome, Shitou tells seekers, and you will see this clearly for yourself. And you can do it because "your essential mind is still and completely whole, and its ability to respond to circumstances is limitless."

This is what Shitou taught. Could there be more encouraging news for us during times of sorrow, misfortune, and pain? We are capable of receiving *anything* with complete equanimity, as long as we look at this anything with a still mind, not through the lens of illusion. Training ourselves to remain grounded in this way is the foundational work of Zen, which is why it requires such discipline and commitment. It is so easy to run away from misfortune and pain, to become inflamed by it, to blame it on others, to try to avoid it, distract from it, gloss over it, or ignore it. This is not the Way, Shitou tells us. Hold your ground with a still mind, be with it, and you will realize your limitless abilities to respond to anything with equanimity. This receiving and responding flows throughout Zen literature as insight to be directly practiced, for enlightenment is found in the back-and-forth responses to life's movement, not outside it. Most of the time we do not receive reality as it is, caught up as we are with the ignorant mind's likes and dislikes, stories and distractions. But it is the Way. Why not see for yourself? Perhaps Shitou is right; perhaps one *is* able to respond to life's circumstances with limitless equanimity. Shitou's way of encouraging his disciples to be with reality was, however, quite different from Mazu's. Mazu, it will be recalled, usually didn't even allow a student to verbalize a problem or ask a question; he just cut it off with a blow or a mighty shout. Shitou engaged. It is hard to imagine him shouting or kicking. Rather, he met the questioner on the questioner's grounds and, with another question as a response, asked the person to look at his or her givens:

QUESTIONER: What about liberation?
THE MASTER: Who binds you?

QUESTIONER: What am I supposed to do?
THE MASTER Why are you asking me?

QUESTIONER Where else can I find what I'm looking for?
THE MASTER: Are you sure you lost it?

Brilliant responses, quietly said, allowing no room for an answer. Both Mazu and Shitou left their students speechless but in different ways. Which way is better? Well, neither of course, for it is the one teaching—everything is empty, so what problem can you possibly have? Neither way is better; both ways are necessary. As noted earlier, it was said that one was not a fully formed meditation practitioner unless one had practiced with both of these masters and their two different approaches, approaches Zen students need to be cognizant of today. Sometimes one needs to cut off the ignorant mind, sometimes one needs to engage it. Knowing which approach to use is the "skillful means" learned with a Zen teacher in the interview (*dokusan/daisan*) room.

THIS IS HOW SHITOU LIVED for twenty-two years—independent, iconoclastic, as confident in his essential practice as was Mazu. When one of the Buddhist temples in the mountains invited him to live there, he declined, preferring solitude to what he saw as the distractions of the monastery. How refreshing it must have been to visit him in his small hut. How invigorating to question him about the Dharma and be left speechless. No wonder many came. Eventually, however, bending to the wishes of his followers, and perhaps compassionately sensing the need for his teaching to be expressed in a more urban setting, Shitou moved to the city of Liangduan in 764, the year the An Lushan rebellion ended. A Zen center grew up around him here, and he attracted even more disciples through encouraging words such as those found in a lecture, excerpted here, that has survived: "Zen Master Xiqian [Shitou] entered the hall and addressed the monks, saying... 'Just see what the Buddha saw. This mind is buddha mind... You should each recognize your miraculous mind.'"

"Recognize your miraculous mind!" Shitou entreats us. Notice your miraculous mind, acknowledge your miraculous mind, acknowledge who you really are, acknowledge that your everyday mind is not different from buddha mind, from awakened mind, from what humans over the ages have called god mind, or divine mind. Acknowledge this, for it is true—and then live it out. But do we acknowledge it? Do we dare to? Do we even dare to think that it might be true? Probably not, for most of us continue to be caught in a dualistic mindset—me and other, human and divine, absolute and relative—living out our discriminating mind's definition of reality as always being separate from the unknowable reality we call "the divine." We tend to see the divine as something beyond ourselves, and so we keep ourselves at a distance from the essential divine self that we really are. This dualistic mindset is how Shakyamuni Buddha saw reality until, through developed discipline and enormous effort, he stilled his discriminating mind and realized he was not separate from anything else. He realized that he, indeed, was not separate from absolute or essential reality. He lived out, practiced, and taught this profound realization for the rest of his life—a realization transmitted through the centuries and the very heart of Zen—and, certainly, the heart of Shitou's teaching.

Shitou's recorded teaching is rather slim but, oh, how splendid. There are a few anecdotal stories of encounters with his students, the lecture excerpted above (which was probably given at the urban monastic center) and two great poems, "The Identity of Relative and Absolute" and the less-well-known "Song of the Grass Roof Hermitage." That is the sum of his recorded output. Yet out of this small record and this largely hermetic life, Shitou's teaching has inspired countless generations of Zen teachers and practitioners. Out of his Dharma grew not only the Caodong (J. Soto) school of Zen, still flourishing to this day, but also two other schools which subsequently died out—the Yunmen (J. Ummon) and the Fayan (J. Hogen) schools. What was it about Shitou's teaching that allowed the Dharma to unfold in such a fruitful way?

For possible answers to this question, it is illuminating to look at Shitou's "Song of the Grass Roof Hermitage," an excerpt of which opened this chapter. Written when he was an old man, the poem holds the essence not only of his teaching but of Shitou's lifestyle and ultimately the man himself. Here is a translation by Taigen Dan Leighton with Yi Wu:

> I've built a grass hut where there's nothing of value.
> After eating, I relax and enjoy a nap.
> When it was completed, fresh weeds appeared.
> Now it's been lived in—covered by weeds.
> The person in the hut lives here calmly,
> not stuck to inside, outside, or in-between.
> Places worldly people live, he doesn't live.
> Realms worldly people love, he doesn't love.
> Though the hut is small, it includes the entire world.
> In ten square feet, an old man illumines forms and their nature.
> A Mahayana bodhisattva trusts without doubt.

The middling and lowly can't help wondering;
Will this hut perish or not?
Perishable or not, the original master is present,
not dwelling south or north, east or west.
Firmly based on steadiness, it can't be surpassed.
A shining window below the green pines—
jade palaces or vermilion towers can't compare with it.
Just sitting with head covered all things are at rest.
Thus, this mountain monk doesn't understand at all.
Living here he no longer works to get free.
Who would proudly arrange seats, trying to entice guests?
Turn around the light to shine within, then just return.
The vast inconceivable source can't be faced or turned away from.
Meet the ancestral teachers, be familiar with their instruction,
bind grasses to build a hut and don't give up.
Let go of hundreds of years and relax completely.
Open your hands and walk, innocent.
Thousands of words, myriad interpretations
are only to free you from obstructions.
If you want to know the undying person in the hut,
don't separate from this skin bag here and now.

In the opening lines of this poem, which surely could be a metaphor for his life, Shitou speaks of "nothing of value"—no-thing or no-body—living there ("a sage has no self"). The teaching is: Don't be attached to things, including the self. This nobody eats, relaxes and naps, lives an ordinary life, and lives it in an enjoyable, balanced way. Could Shitou have been addressing the ascetic seekers in the mountains in their need to gain something? Possibly. From the vantage point of his many years of deep practice, from his clear seeing into the true nature of reality, isn't he telling seekers not to be attached to nonattachment, not to seek enlightenment outside of life, and not to forget their bodies? Isn't he telling us, as well? We must always remember that it is our body that meditates, eats, sleeps, creates, works, and relaxes, and that these activities need to be carried out in a balanced way—not too little, not too much. As the Parayana Sutra puts it, the practice of the path is "present moment awareness to the body."

Maintaining this balance is one of the greatest challenges lay Zen practitioners have today. Monastic life has its hardships for sure, but at least the structure of a balanced life exists in monastery schedules, as it does during retreats. Structuring a balanced life for ourselves in today's world, without such an outward guide and bombarded from all sides with so much to do, we must seek to make such a schedule for ourselves in order to be constantly reminded that to eat, work, create, relax, and sleep are all "holy endeavors."

So we must practice the Middle Way, practice the realization that we are both human and divine. We do this not by fighting our humanity, but by not getting caught by it. And this practice never ends because, as the poem goes on, the hut is constantly sprouting weeds. Is Shitou troubled by the weeds? Does he fight them? Is he trying to get rid of them? Apparently not. The weeds are part of the hut, part of his life. Do we allow them to be part of ours? Or do we fight with our humanity, our greed, hatred, and ignorance that are, as the Gatha of Repentance puts it, "beginningless"? We can't fight with our humanity just as we can't fight with the thoughts that arise during zazen. It is a hopeless battle.

The poet goes on to say that he lives in the here and now, not seeking to be somewhere else. For "though the hut is small, it includes the entire world." From the point of view of Oneness, which was Shitou's perspective, just this "ten square feet" was everything, it was nature illumined, it was enough, and he trusted this without doubt. Do we illumine nature by practicing awareness of this moment, as it is here and now? Is it enough? Or do we doubt the now, find the present to be unpalatable, not to our liking, not enough? Is our present usually subsumed by the desire for something else, something more, somewhere else? Striving to live in the present is an urgent part of Zen practice because living in the moment and trusting it is life. And, strangely, it is preparation for death, because death and all it is imagined to be is just an idea. To live in the present without any imagining of death is the liberation offered by a still mind that has no further questions, and needs no further answers about the matter.

The Great Matter of life and death must certainly have been raised by those who came to see Shitou, for he notes that "the middling and the lowly can't help wondering, will this hut perish or not?" That is our wondering, is it not? What happens when I die? What is death? What does it mean? "I don't know," Shitou answers us.

> Daowu asked, "What is the great meaning of the buddha-dharma?"
> Shitou said, "Not attaining. Not knowing."

I don't know what happens when one dies, Shitou might say, but it is not a problem because "the original master" is always present. Our essential self (the original master), without beginning and end, is present in this moment, whatever this moment may look like. Live the now, this great poem is telling us, and you'll be just fine. Stop worrying (by practicing stilling the worrying mind), stop trying to understand death (by practicing stilling the need-to-understand mind), stop attaining (by practicing stilling the have-to-attain mind). The original master cannot *not* be present. You and your essence are not two. See as the Buddha saw. This reality cannot be surpassed—how can you surpass *One?* It is "a shining window below the green pines—jade palaces or vermilion towers can't compare with it."

These two lines are probably the most poetic in this beautiful poem and reflect an important aspect of Zen that came out of China, namely the spirit of the poet. "A shining window below the green pines" is not a phrase that would be found in the more didactic writing of the Indian sutras. Yet Chinese writers and artists—such as Wang Wei, the great poet who lived at the time of Shitou and who practiced Zen—greatly influenced the direction that the Buddha Way took in China (and subsequently in Japan, where art as an integral part of the Zen way reached its pinnacle). Wang Wei was at the height of his fame during Shitou's time in the mountains, and, given the nature of his poetry, it is easy to imagine copies of his work or the work of other poets tucked away somewhere in that small hut on the rock. All this reminds us that poetry, music, and art are deep expressions of our essentialness and we would do well to develop them, not just through the way of calligraphy and haiku but through all available Western art forms as well. Yes, what can surpass "a shining window below the green pines"? The stuff we accumulate cannot compare, the stuff we desire cannot compare. "Just sitting with head covered all things are at rest." Just sitting, just walking, just eating, just working, just creating—in the now—all things are at rest.

And "I don't understand any of it," Shitou says. What's more, I don't need to understand it, he might have added. I no longer need to *become* free, to seek liberation, for "the vast inconceivable source can't be faced or turned away from" since it *is* me. You can't face yourself or turn away from yourself because you're *it*. What do you need to understand? Can the eye see itself? "Meet the ancestral teachers [for they are you], be familiar with their instruction [for it is yours], bind grasses to build a hut [take care of your body, your mind, this life] and don't give up."

Don't give up! Surely this quiet man is speaking to you and me, encouraging us because he has known how difficult this path is and has seen how easy it is to give up. Don't give up the practice of stilling the mind, but at the same time relax completely—the paradox of Zen. "Walk, innocent." Live simply. Everything is complete right now. Don't give up! Don't give up trusting yourself. And don't let the words of the Dharma complicate things for you, for "thousands of words, myriad interpretations are only to free you from obstructions." As "The Identity of Relative and Absolute" says, "Reading words, you should grasp the great reality." Trust yourself and see beyond.

In closing, Shitou returns once again to the great Heart Sutra truth—that "emptiness is *exactly* form, form is *exactly* emptiness"—when he writes, "If you want to know the undying person in the hut [absolute self] don't separate from this skin bag [relative self] here and now."

He never did. Shitou died in 790, two years after Mazu's passing. He was ninety years old.

He never gave up. Why should we?

5. GUISHAN

J. ISAN 771–853

THERE ARE MANY WHO ATTAIN THE GREAT POTENTIAL, BUT FEW WHO REALIZE THE GREAT FUNCTION

AN AWAKENED ZEN LIFE is one that expresses right insight through right action. Seeing into the true nature of reality is not complete until that reality begins to shape our daily life into one that is less controlled by old, conditioned, selfish habits of greed, anger, hatred, and ignorance, and more given over to the selfless living of the oneness of all that is. Right action is at the heart of the Buddha's Noble Eightfold Path of Awakening, for, as he taught, action is the expression of right thought and right meditation. All too often, however, practitioners believe that grasping the truth of the Dharma is enough. It is not. Enlightenment isn't fully realized until it is expressed in our lives—until it functions. The two great masters who shaped Zen in the eighth century, Mazu and Shitou, both emphasized functioning of insight in their life and teaching. Mazu's Dharma grandson Guishan Lingyou (J. Isan Reiyu) developed it further.

Guishan was born in Changxi, the capital of Fuzhou Province, in 771, when both Mazu and Shitou were still alive and teaching vigorously. His name at birth was Lingyou and his family name was Cho. The record tells us that Guishan left his parents when he was fifteen, studied in a local monastery under a Vinaya master, and later received ordination after further Vinaya study at another Buddhist center. Vinaya—rules and disciplines based on moral precepts, which governed the life of Buddhist monks and nuns—had evolved from the rules and disciplines of the original sangha of Siddhartha Gautama, the Buddha, founded in the sixth century BCE. Over time, these regulations had grown and eventually developed into the Vinaya school of Buddhism so that, by the time Guishan was born, Vinaya played a major role in all Buddhist monasteries in China.

This is important to note, for Guishan's teaching would be based on adherence to a strict moral code. Here is what he later wrote in his Admonitions: "The Buddha first defined precepts to begin to remove the veils of ignorance. With standards and refinements of conduct pure as ice and snow, the precepts rein and concentrate the minds of beginners in respect to what to stop, what to uphold, what to do and what not to do. Their details reform every kind of crudity and decadence. How can you understand the supreme vehicle of complete meaning without having paid heed to moral principles? Beware of spending a lifetime in vain; later regrets are useless."

People today often believe that ethics and morality play no part in Zen training—that Zen is about meditation only. The passage quoted above proves this to be false. Right meditation does bring about right living, but the ego-mind can so easily be conditioned by false information that outer guidelines are also needed to direct us. Such guidelines are called precepts. They are meant to be standards—not laws but standards— and today the receiving of the precepts (*jukai* as it is called in Japanese Zen) is the ceremony in which a lay practitioner officially commits to the upholding of the precepts to the best of his or her ability as an outward sign of being a follower of the Way.

The original precepts of the Vinaya were numerous and complicated and so, in the Mahayana tradition of Zen, were eventually distilled into sixteen. The first three—taking refuge in Buddha, taking refuge in Dharma, taking refuge in Sangha—are the same as those taken by Chinese Zen monks over one thousand years ago during their ceremony of ordination. Likewise, the first five of what are known as the ten grave precepts are the same as those the monks vowed to follow: not killing, not stealing, not misusing sexuality, not lying, not being subject to intoxicants. The last five of the ten grave precepts, however, are charmingly different. Today's last five—not talking about others, not inflating oneself, not being angry, not being stingy, and upholding the "Three Treasures" of Buddha, Dharma, Sangha—replaced admonitions to not sleep on a high and wide bed, to not wear necklaces or hair ornaments (it is hard to imagine how one could wear a hair ornament if one's head was shaved, but there it is), to not watch theatrical singing or dancing, to not carry gold or coins, and to not eat at unauthorized times. Everything changes—even some precept standards!

So Guishan studied the sutras and assiduously practiced the Vinaya. Then, at the age of twenty-three, something momentous happened. He traveled to Jiangxi Province, to a very steep mountain called Baizhang, just south of the Yangtze River, to meet with the abbot of the monastery there. The abbot too was named Baizhang—Baizhang Huaihai (J. Hyakujo Ekai)—for, as noted previously, Zen masters (with the exception of Mazu) took the name of their locality rather than keeping their family names. (This was probably a sign of humility on a master's part but must have also been a handy way to find a particular teacher— find his mountain or province and then just ask around.) Baizhang was Mazu's first Dharma successor and, shortly after Mazu's death in 788, he had moved to Mount Baizhang, where generous supporters helped build a monastery. Just as this monastery and its new Zen monastic code were being established, Guishan arrived. The record does not tell us why he was drawn to a Zen teacher but drawn he was, and the teacher he chose was one who was to affect Zen in a profound way.

Nelson Foster and Jack Shoemaker, in their book *The Roaring Stream*, give us a succinct overview of Buddhism at the beginning of the eighth century: "At this time, lines among Buddhist schools remained quite blurry; in many respects, they were still different teachings more than different sects. Movement among the country's five thousand Buddhist monasteries and temples was quite free, and, as students and lecturers circulated, they carried texts, ideas, metaphors, teaching methods, and the like, creating an active exchange among diverse traditions." Buddhism was fluid; it was growing and it had no central authority. This alarmed Emperor Xuanzong (the same emperor who was to later suffer in the An Lushan rebellion, described in the previous two chapters), and in 729 he decreed that all monks and nuns were to be registered, thus bringing about greater government control over the Buddhist community. Government control, however, had its rewards, for it brought financial support from the government, and Buddhist groups soon began to define and differentiate themselves in hopes of receiving the fruits of state patronage. It was during this time that the Zen community began to define itself (though many of its teachers shunned the court and its trappings) and eventually Baizhang became its major definer. He did this not so much through doctrines and methods (though he was a brilliant teacher) but by formulating a particular set of monastic rules known as the Baizhang Zen Monastic Regulations.

Up until then, meditation-oriented masters and their disciples had either been guests in Buddhist monasteries (primarily of the Vinaya school) or were part of loosely formed meditating communities. We must remember that the "finished product" we know as Zen was at the beginning of the ninth century simply a form of Buddhism that emphasized meditation. All Buddhists practiced meditation but Zen's emphasis on meditation was total—a meditation beyond words and silence. Though there is evidence to suggest that some masters, like Hongren and his successor Huineng, as well as Huineng's Dharma grandson Mazu, were developing monastic centers that emphasized meditation, Zen was not yet a distinct and separate entity. This all changed with Baizhang. At the end of the eighth century he began to formulate Zen's rules and forms, based on what was happening at the above-mentioned monasteries, which eventually led to the formation of independent Zen communities.

Why should we care today how Zen came to be defined or why the development of the Zen monastic regulations was so important? What does it have to do with our practice today? A great deal, in fact. We would not be practicing today if structure and systemization had not been put in place at the end of the eighth century. As Martin Collcutt writes in *Five Mountains*, "Although the disciplined character of Zen community life is frequently ignored in discussions of the history of Zen, the existence of a strict, clearly defined yet flexible rule gave strength and longevity to the Chan schools in China." These rules, established by Baizhang and handed down from generation to generation, were honed, refined, and adapted for different times and places, moving to Korea and Japan and eventually to the West in the twentieth century. They are now ours, and whether we know it or not we are undeniably involved in our own version of them, creating forms and rituals that today no longer primarily serve a monastic culture but support the modern lay culture of the twenty-first century. When our time has passed, we, like the Golden Age masters, will be history, as new Zen cultures adapt what we developed and make it their own. It is the movement of the Dharma, flowing like an endless river.

The original text of the Baizhang Zen Monastic Regulations no longer exists but numerous references to it are made in what are known as the Chongning Monastic Regulations, compiled at the beginning of the twelfth century. Recently translated from the Chinese as *The Baizhang Zen Monastic Regulations*, it was the foundation on which all future Zen monastic life was built. A fascinating work, it offers a window into the lives of all those countless, sometimes hapless monks we encounter in the koans as they ask masters their Zen questions, only to be stunned into paralyzed silence by their irrational answers. Who were these anonymous people with whom we so often identify when we, like they, struggle through the frustrations of the practice? How did they live? Under what conditions did they awaken? Well, the Regulations offer us what could be called unsung heroic models of Zen determination. The practice of the Way was not easy; it demanded sacrifice, hard work, and true devotion, as can be seen in the descriptions of Zen communal life below. And the practice of the Way is still not easy. The times may be different, but we can never forget that awakening still demands sacrifice, hard work, and true devotion, whether inside or outside of a monastery.

In developing the Regulations, Baizhang showed himself to be not only a person of prodigious organizational skills but also one who trusted his own inner vision and had the confidence to carry it out. As the leader of his monastery, he discarded those parts of the Indian monastic code that no longer worked, replacing them with practical rules that supported the needs of the monks in his care. *The Transmission of the Lamp* lists some of the major changes Baizhang instituted:

▶ The monks were now to live in the same space in which they meditated—not in separate buildings—and meditation platforms were built along the sides of the monks' hall with a place for personal belongings. This new kind of physical space must have reinforced the primacy of meditation in a very tangible way.

▶ Monks' seniority was established not according to their social status but according to their length of time at the monastery—surely quite a blow to hierarchy and its privileges.

▶ Building upon the one-on-one exchanges between Mazu and his students, monks now regularly went to have private meetings with the master in his room (for *dokusan* or *daisan*).

▶ The community gathered in the morning and evening to hear the Dharma talk (for which they evidently stood) and then, in a new development, engaged the master in debate.

In quite a significant move, manual labor was also introduced. It was to become a major characteristic of the Zen Buddhist school—setting it apart from all other Buddhist sects. *The Transmission of the Lamp* tells us that everyone in the community had to work equally, and "ten offices or chambers" were set up, each with its own supervising monk who made sure the work was carried out diligently. Baizhang participated in the communal work along with everyone else and coined the famous teaching, "A day without work is a day without food." Manual labor must have already been in place in some Zen monasteries, as many of them were far off the beaten track, and if everyone didn't cooperate in the growing, harvesting, and preparation of their food they may not have eaten. In such cases, manual labor seems to have been a necessity. But to make it an official part of the monastic rule (no matter where a monastery was located) must have been truly radical. Till then Buddhist monks had been forbidden by the Vinaya to do manual labor of any kind because the first precept forbade the killing of any creature (even insects), something that would have invariably happened if the soil was tilled. So slaves (yes, slaves), prisoners, or indentured farmers did the dirty work, including the killing (leaving one to wonder whether the monks realized that they were simply passing the buck).

Baizhang obviously saw through this double standard and out of his insight must also have seen that without working for their food monks were not participating in the ordinary tasks of life. By introducing manual labor as a major component of Zen, he brought to full flower Mazu's Dharma of "functioning." Insight is not enough, it must be connected to one's life, and Baizhang was willing to break the rules of Vinaya to express this teaching. A modern Zen master, Robert Aitken, put it this way in his book *Mind of Clover*: "Without *samu* [work practice], Zen Buddhism would be a cult, isolated form daily life... *Samu* is the extension of meditation to its function."

In another move of significance, Baizhang did away with the Buddha hall (the place where services and ceremonial functions were held) because, as *The Transmission of the Lamp* put it, "not to construct a Buddha hall but only to build a Dharma hall is to demonstrate a proper respect for the abbot as the mind-to-mind inheritor of the teachings of Buddha and the Chan patriarchs." Martin Collcott writes in *Five Mountains* that there were four basic reasons for the rejection of the Buddha hall. "A strong strand of iconoclasm in Chan thought, a sense of Chan sectarian identity, a fear that energy would be drawn from meditation and Zen practice into elaborate ceremonial functions in the Buddha hall (involving a shift from the struggle to attain enlightenment by one's own efforts to reliance on prayers and devotions) and, finally, a fear that, through these ceremonies, dependence on the state and the patrons who sponsored the Buddha hall ceremonies and memorial services would be unduly increased."

All in all, Baizhang's monastic regulations helped forge the "Zen way," which came to be defined by its four principal components: meditation, Dharma talks, one-to-one meetings with the teacher, and work practice. These four defining components hold to this day. Yes, Baizhang was radical. He took steps that broke with the ancient rules of Vinaya, trusted his own instincts, and set up new forms that helped seekers of the day to awaken, freeing them from ancient traditions that no longer worked. As Zen expands in the West, are we not engaged in similar radical steps? Women, for the first time in more than 2,500 years, are being accepted as formal teachers; the role of feelings and emotions in practitioners' lives is more and more becoming part of teaching (if Zen is your life, are not feelings and emotions part of that life?); the supportive role of modern therapeutic processes is being accepted; the difficulties inherent in lay practice, such as work, family responsibilities, and living far from teachers and meditation centers are being addressed; and the role of social activism (Engaged Buddhism as it is often called) is being explored.

But might we go further? As Zen expresses itself through its emerging lay, Western voice, might it be helpful for us to question some of the forms and traditions of its monastic, Asian roots to see whether they do or do not work for us? Why, for example, do English- or French- or German-speaking people chant the Heart Sutra (and other chants) in Japanese or Korean? Did the Japanese chant the sutras in Chinese? Did the Koreans? Did the Chinese chant them in Sanskrit? Might it be helpful for Western practitioners to know the meaning of what they are chanting, as did the Indians, Chinese, Koreans, and Japanese? And why, for example, do lay people in some Zen communities put on monks' robes to meditate if they are not monks? Do robes help the lay practitioner or might they risk separating zazen from the twenty-four-hour-a-day practice it is meant to be by making zazen something special and separate in some people's minds? Certainly there are many good reasons to maintain and treasure our Zen traditions; ultimately one way is not better or worse than another. It is only that doing things simply because they are part of a tradition without asking whether this tradition helps us in our journey today does not seem to be the way that Baizhang and other masters of Zen's Golden Age addressed the traditions of their time.

Baizhang's monastic rules soon began to be adopted by other Zen masters as they formed their own communities; the monasteries described in the chapters of this book that follow would have looked remarkably similar to Baizhang's place. Of course, what probably began as quite a simple set of rules soon began to grow and grow, as such things are wont to do. By the beginning of the twelfth century, the

Monastic Regulations had become quite extensive, offering sections such as "The Serving of Tea on the Occasion of the Transfer of Duties Between the Former and New Dual Order Officials." Baizhang, always so simple and direct, would probably not have approved. On the whole, however, his spirit is in the Regulations, and so too is the spirit of his disciple, Guishan.

GUISHAN HAD BEEN GIVEN food preparation duties in the kitchen shortly after his arrival at the monastery and because of this it seems safe to assume that he was directly involved in creating some of the work regulations in Baizhang's code. The twelfth-century Monastic Regulations give a full description of the tasks of the "Kitchen Official," detailing, among other things, how rice gruel was to be served in the morning and at noon, how sanitary standards were to be maintained and thrift to be kept, and how novices working in the kitchen were to be strongly supervised. It was a full-time job—it was full-time "functioning." The service of the cook eventually came to hold a special place in the monastic order. The great Japanese Zen master Dogen had his first awakening through the insights of a Zen cook whom he met soon after his arrival in China.

When we just function, just act, just work, with no idea of a "me" that is functioning or acting or working, the Dharma is fully expressed, for then there is no separation. Although things are accomplished in the relative sense (cause and effect), there are no results in the absolute sense (no cause and no effect), for, in the reality of not-two, functioning is simply the pure expression of that which we call "it" or "thusness." This is one of the most difficult truths to grasp, much less to carry out, and it is why work practice is such an essential part of Zen training. Work practice periods are built into the daily structure of all Zen centers and are an integral part of all meditation retreats not merely because they are practical (household tasks are, after all, necessary) but because they help practitioners live and function in the world with a still mind, detached from placing meanings of greater or less importance on any one thing. Zen is not limited to the meditation mat; Zen is sweeping, cooking, and cleaning as well, and work practice offers us the opportunity to practice this regularly in the zendo setting so that we can then extend such mindful practice into our daily lives.

How do *you* view work practice? Is it a duty to be performed at the end of a sitting session? How do you view work? Is it a burden for you in one way or another, something to be endured until you can escape into the relief of the evening, the weekend, or the meditation mat? Are the daily chores around your home seeming impediments that keep you from more "interesting" pursuits? Do you undertake such chores with a heavy sigh, postpone them as much as possible, carry them out in a sloppy way? If so, Master Guishan is addressing you when he says, "Beware of spending a lifetime in vain; later regrets are useless." Work and home chores *are* the Way. Pay attention! And the place to begin seeing work and chores in this new light is at the zendo, to participate fully when work practice is assigned. Cleaning the bathroom or chopping the onions is no less important than sitting in deep meditation. Grasping this and acting on it is called waking up. It is what Guishan did for twenty years.

After his arrival at Baizhang's monastery, Guishan (at this point still called Lingyou) was accepted by Baizhang as a disciple and soon became one of his leading students. One day, while serving as Baizhang's attendant, the master asked him who he was. "Lingyou," was the reply. There may have been a pause. "Can you see if there's any burning charcoal in the fire pot?" Baizhang asked. Guishan did so. "No, there's no burning charcoal there," he said. Baizhang rose, took the poker, poked deep into the fire, and pulled out a small piece of burning charcoal. "Isn't this a burning charcoal?" he asked. Guishan was awakened. Baizhang said, "In the scripture it says, 'If you want to understand the meaning of buddha nature, then you should look in the realm of temporal causation.'" In other words, buddha does not exist as emptiness (the nonburning fire pot); buddha is always "burning"—in this case as Lingyou. Likewise, Lingyou did not exist as Lingyou; Lingyou was always "burning"—as buddha. Baizhang went on to say, "When it [buddha nature] expresses itself, it is like...remembering something that was forgotten and realizing that the self and other things do not come from someplace else."

"Remembering something that was forgotten." Isn't this an apt description of insight?

At the deepest level, are we not seeking something ancient and profound that we somehow sense is there but cannot seem to access? Is it not accessed when our discriminating ego-mind is stilled and we have a moment of insight, when the clouds part, so to speak, and we see as if for the first time? But is it the first time? Or is it something remembered? Has it not always been us? And has it not been our ego-mind that placed "it"—whatever we imagine "it" to be—someplace else? "Enlightenment," Baizhang went on to say, "is just this mind that does not hold to ideas of emptiness, delusion, mundane, or sacred." Emptiness, he was saying, is just functioning—just living your life. It is the hardest of truths for us to accept, for our minds constantly want to separate sacred from mundane. However, we must not only accept this truth, but live it because, as Baizhang concluded, "Having arrived at this, you must uphold and sustain it." And sustain it is what Guishan did. He remained with Baizhang for many years and during all that time he served in the kitchen as the cook (*tenzo* as it is called in Japanese Zen), just functioning.

Then one day around the year 814, as recounted in *The Transmission of the Lamp*, a Buddhist mendicant from Hunan Province named Sima visited the monastery. He told Baizhang that on a certain mountain called Gui resided many worthy practitioners who needed a teacher. When Baizhang asked if he himself should go to Mount Gui, the pilgrim replied that this was not a good idea. "Why not?" asked the ninety-four-year-old Baizhang. (What a warrior!) "Because you are a teacher of bone; that place is the flesh." In other words, the pilgrim might as well have said, "because you are too gaunt, too ascetic, too old, and these devoted practitioners need new blood." "Well," said Baizhang, obviously bowing to the limitations of his age, "is there anyone here at my place who could take on the leadership position on Mount Gui?" "Let me examine those whom you think might be worthy and I'll see," said Sima. So the master summoned the head monk, whose name was Hua. Sima had him speak a few words and walk back and forth, and then said, "He won't do." So Baizhang summoned Guishan (still called Lingyou). Sima took one look at him and said, "This is the right person to be abbot of Mount Gui." Later that evening, Baizhang called Lingyou to his room and told him he would be going to Mount Gui to "carry on my teaching for future generations." When Hua heard of this he went indignantly to the master. "I'm the head monk," he said. "Why is the head cook going to be abbot?" Good question. After all, Sima the pilgrim had given no reason for his choice and neither had Baizhang. So the master told Hua that he would give him a test in front of the whole assembly to determine if he should, after all, become the abbot. All the monks were summoned the next day and the test was administered. It remains with us to this day as koan 40 in *The Gateless Gate*.

Baizhang placed a water bucket in front of Hua. "You can't call it a water bucket. What do you call it?" "You can't call it a wooden stool," said the head monk. Not bad, Baizhang may have thought. He then called Lingyou and asked him the same question. Lingyou kicked over the bucket and walked out. Baizhang laughed out loud. "The head monk loses," he cried. The head cook was to be the new abbot, and this is how Lingyou became Guishan of Mount Gui.

Functioning does not require words, it requires action. By kicking over the water bucket, Guishan acknowledged its existence (form), and by kicking it over he acknowledged its nonexistence (emptiness). What water bucket? What abbotship? Let me get back to mixing the rice gruel! (Those who don't seek positions and titles are the ones that Zen masters pay attention to when seeking to fill such positions.) And what about head monk Hua? One trusts he gained insight into the truth that the head monk is not better than the head cook—and vice versa.

Baizhang died in 814. It is not clear whether Guishan stayed with his teacher until then but around that time, he set out to assume his new responsibilities, taking with him Baizhang's *hossu*, the master's flywhisk (a horsetail attached to a pole), which he had received from Baizhang as a sign of Dharma transmission. (How very practical of the Chinese masters—to make the sign of the master's teaching authority double as a tool to whisk away flies!) Mount Gui was very steep and largely inaccessible, and "only monkeys could be found for companions and only chestnuts were available as food." It was to this place that Guishan traveled and where he began to teach in what must have been very primitive conditions. When people at the foot of the mountain heard that he was living there, they banded together and built him a monastery up on the steep slopes. Many began to join him there to learn and be inspired.

Notable among those who came was Yangshan Huiji (J. Kyozan Ejaku), who was to become Guishan's principal disciple. Yangshan had been opened to the wisdom of Zen with another teacher so that by the time he arrived on Mount Gui his insight was quite deep. He came to full enlightenment under Guishan when one day he grasped in an instant the truth of Guishan's words: "When thoughts are exhausted you've arrived at the source where true nature is revealed as eternally abiding. In that place, there is no difference between affairs (world) and principle (source), and the true Buddha is manifested."

Yangshan stayed at Guishan's place for about fifteen years and during that time these two awakened human beings lived their days in what Zen calls "the practice of the enlightened." It is important to note the word "practice" here. Enlightenment is not a one-time thing as so many who come to Zen erroneously believe. Yes, it is sudden and complete in the moment that our awareness opens up and we get it. But this awareness must be cultivated, as Guishan's Dharma grandfather, Mazu, famously taught. Enlightenment must be practiced, for practice is the only way enlightenment is maintained. Without practice or cultivation, the clouds of ignorance cover up enlightenment awareness quickly. Guishan and Yangshan practiced. They expressed their essential nature in the simple functioning of their lives as they carried out their monastic duties—herding cows, plowing fields, harvesting crops, washing clothes, picking tea leaves, and so forth—not getting caught in either absolute or relative. There is no difference between affairs of the world and the source. No difference.

One of the "work practice dialogues" of these two masters (now koan 15 in *The Book of Equanimity*) expresses this enlightened living:

"Where have you come from?" Guishan asked Yangshan.

"From the fields."

"How many people were in the fields?"

Yangshan stuck his hoe into the ground and just stood there with his hands across his chest.

"In the southern mountains, there are many people reaping thatch," said Guishan.

Yangshan pulled out his hoe and left.

"WHERE HAVE YOU COME FROM?" There is nowhere to "come from" in the absolute sense and yet in the relative sense there is. Yangshan maintains his relative ground—the fields. "How many people in the fields?" In the relative sense, there are indeed people in the fields but Yangshan maintains his absolute ground. What people? There is only here. Yet there *are* people reaping. Of course. I'm off. No difference between affairs of the world and the source. Source and function, absolute and relative, emptiness and form are not the same and yet are the same. Fully realizing their precisely different sameness is enlightenment. Living out their precisely different sameness is enlightened living. What a challenge, right? What a practice!

Living out such practice, these two great teachers passed down a style of teaching that came to be called the Guiyang school—the first of the Five Schools of Zen—named after both of them. The school died out after five generations but the compassionate teaching of its founders remains alive and vibrant. Guishan taught on Mount Gui for about forty years and eventually became the most prominent Zen master of his time in southern China. He had forty-one Dharma successors, and Zen practitioners may be interested to know that one of them, Master Xingyan Zhixian (J. Kyogen Chikan), is the fellow who came up with that ultimate dilemma koan of the "man up the tree"—koan 5 in *The Gateless Gate*. A man is hanging on to a tree branch by his teeth. Another man comes along and asks him the meaning of Zen. If the man in the tree keeps holding on, he won't answer the question. If he answers it, he will die. At such a moment, what would you do? asks Guishan's Dharma heir, Master Xingyan. If you've struggled with that koan, you now know who to blame for your frustration.

Guishan is also known for being one of the few Zen masters to have a documented female disciple, a nun nicknamed Iron Grindstone Liu because of the sharpness of her insight and her ability to respond dramatically in Dharma exchanges. She couldn't be fooled, as *The Blue Cliff Record* commentary puts it. Liu lived in a hermitage near Guishan's monastery and had awakened as his student. The relationship between the two was mutually respectful and, from the recorded exchange between Liu and the master that has been handed down to us as koan 24 in *The Blue Cliff Record*, it is clear that they were peers who loved to "Zen joust."

Liu comes to visit her teacher and, on entering the room, Guishan (who was known as "Old Buffalo") greets her with, "Ah, Old Female Buffalo, so you're here." Liu springs her question. "Tomorrow there's a big festival on Mount Taishan [a sacred mountain, six hundred miles away and impossible to reach in a day], are you going?" Guishan lies down on the floor ("I'm already there"). Liu leaves. This is a perfect example of the unspoken language of two Zen adepts who surely must have delighted in each other's insight whenever they met.

Such mutuality also existed between the master and other future major Zen teachers who came to study with him. Chief among them was Deshan Xuanjian (J. Tokusan Senkan), who, as we shall see in a later chapter, had a dramatic encounter with Guishan's *hossu*, and Yunyan Tansheng (J. Ungan Donjo), teacher of Dongshan Liangjie (J. Tozan Ryokai), whom we will also meet later.

"What is the seat of enlightenment?" Guishan asked Yunyan.

"Freedom from artificiality," replied Yunyan, and he then asked Guishan the same question: "What is the seat of enlightenment?"

"The vanity of all things," replied Guishan.

What an amazing truth, is it not? The imperfections of this world, our imperfections or "vanities," are the seat of enlightenment. To look outside or beyond our human condition for that ineffable which we can only call "it" is folly. Just here, just now, as is—"absolute" functioning.

This is the truth that Guishan taught and practiced vigorously and compassionately on his steep mountain for forty years. Out of this he sought to develop a community of equally compassionate persons.

"When you deeply know your faults and suffering," he told his students, "then you can encourage each other to persevere with your practice. Make a vow that for the next hundred eons and thousand lives you will everywhere be spiritual companions to each other."

Zen Master Guishan's life affected countless generations, and his disciplined, kind, and generous spirit continues to speak to us today. He could have been describing himself when he wrote in his Admonitions:

> When the voice is gentle, the echo corresponds;
> when the figure is upright, the shadow is straight.

6. LINJI

J. RINZAI; D. 867

THE TRUE PERSON OF NO RANK

LINJI YIXUAN (J. Rinzai Gigen), Dharma grandson of Mazu, addressed the assembly, saying, "Bring to rest the thoughts of the ceaselessly seeking mind and you'll not differ from the Patriarch-Buddha. Do you want to know the Patriarch-Buddha? He is none other than you who stand before me listening to my discourse." It is *you*, says Master Linji. You are buddha. You are awakened.

Many people are initially drawn to Zen to find ways to calm the turmoil of their mind, to become more grounded, to be more at peace, to realize deeper self-connection. And all of that eventually happens, to some degree or other. But as one practices, one eventually begins to realize that what Zen really offers is the path, the practical tools, to awaken to the fact of who one truly is. We are *buddhas*, we are awakened—already, now, here, today, just as we are in this moment. We don't *become* awakened; we already are awakened but just don't realize it. To realize it, all we have to do is "bring to rest the thoughts of the ceaselessly seeking mind." That is all we have to do! Simple—and yet, as anyone who has attempted the actualization of this action knows, it is extremely difficult.

One could say that the relentless, in-your-face teaching of "Simple! Just still the ego-mind!" sums up Linji's teaching in the Recorded Sayings of Master Linji, known simply as the Linji-lu. But that is not where he began his spiritual journey, for at the outset he was what one might call orthodox.

75

Linji was born sometime between 810 and 815 in the northern Chinese city of Nanhua, and his family name was Hsing. The memorial inscription that closes the Linji-lu tell us that he was a dutiful child and that, upon receiving ordination as a monk at an early age, he was diligent in his study of the Vinaya, or rules for monastic discipline, as well as the sutras, or Buddhist scriptures. Section 19 of the Linji-lu corroborates this description of Linji's early years, showing him to be an intense, serious, and highly focused young man.

How instructive. This foundational master, so famous for his unrelenting assault on all rules and study (summed up in his almost shocking admonition in section 19 of the Linji-lu, "If you meet a buddha, kill the buddha"), began his exploration of the Way very much with rules and study. Both approaches (rules and study and no rules and no study) were to serve him well; indeed, both serve all Zen practitioners well. While no-form is the essential nature of reality, form is the structure that holds us *in* reality. It is the reason why Zen is such a structured practice, why it insists on punctuality, schedules, and discipline. This structure is provided for our support. All we have to do is show up, accept it, pay attention to it, and follow it. Some people find such structure to be rigid and controlling but when viewed with the clarity of the Zen eye it is seen instead to be a compassionate guide to liberation, for it provides a point of focus for our ever-wandering awareness.

Study, too, was especially important for Linji in his early years, for it opened his vision, deepened his knowledge of the vast scope of the Dharma, and introduced him to the insights of those masterful teachers who came before him, beginning with Shakyamuni Buddha himself. Study is important for us, as well, as long as we know that what we read and study is always someone else's truth; it is our work to realize our own version of that truth by eventually doing what Linji did when he realized that "these [rules and study] are just medicines to cure the sickness of the world." As he writes in the Linji-lu, "Finally, I tossed the teachings aside and sought the Way through Chan practice." Yes, rules and teaching are necessary but ultimately it is with the discipline of Zen meditation that the ego-mind, which seeks "medicines and cures," is stilled. But not without a learning curve. "I had to probe and polish and undergo experiences until one morning I could see clearly for myself."

How did Linji probe and polish? Once he had been introduced to Zen, he left his homeland and traveled around, as was the custom, until he found a monastery and a teacher who fit his need—much like the shopping around people do today. His search came to an end when he found Master Huangbo's monastery south of the Yangtze River. Master Huangbo Xiyun (J. Obaku Kiun) had a distinguished lineage. He was the first Dharma successor of Master Baizhang, and his Dharma brother was Master Guishan. The young, intense Linji was probably attracted to the highly disciplined monastic rule these three men had jointly begun to forge.

Here is what happened at Huangbo's place, as laid out in section 48 of the Linji-lu, as well as in koan 86 of *The Book of Equanimity*. It is one of the great Zen enlightenment stories of all time.

For the first three years, in his usual serious way, Linji diligently carried out all the duties of a monk "in an earnest manner." The head monk, whose name was Muzhou Daoming (J. Bokushu Domyo), began to notice (head monks usually notice those who carry out their service duties diligently) and thought to himself that this young man was different from the others. Muzhou was a demanding head monk who was to become a great Zen master in his own right—we shall meet him again in a later chapter as the catalyst for the rather painful awakening of Yunmen Wenyan (J. Ummon Bun-en). Muzhou approached Linji and after inquiring how long Linji had been there, he asked, "Have you been in to question the master yet?" To which Linji replied, "No, I don't know what to ask." Three years and he had not yet spoken to the teacher!

Once again we see the severe doubt and timidity that grips many who first come to Zen. "I don't know what to ask the teacher. I don't know what I am supposed to say." This self-doubt is based on the erroneous idea that there is something one *should* ask or say. Discovering that there are no "shoulds" in the meeting between teacher and student is one of the great surprises awaiting all who first participate in such an exchange. It is the same today as it was in Linji's time. But one has to find out by doing it, and Linji found out.

On hearing that Linji had never gone to speak with Huangbo, Muzhou, knowing full well what would ensue, said to him, "Well, why not go to the master today and, to kindly help you out, here is a question you can ask: 'What is the meaning of the Buddha's teaching?'" Probably grateful and relieved that he finally had a "real Zen question" to ask, Linji dutifully went to the interview with Huangbo, not knowing he had been sent into the lion's den. After the customary formal greeting he asked his question but to his utter surprise and shock, before he could even finish speaking, Huangbo hit him. (Remember, Huangbo was the Dharma grandson of Mazu, he of the kicks and shouts.) Linji was shaken. He went back to Muzhou who asked him in all innocence, "Well, young monk, how did it go?" Bewildered, Linji related what had happened, adding plaintively, "I don't understand." "Well, go ask him again," said the wily head monk, and this the disciplined but unsuspecting Linji did—three times with the same results.

After the third visit he returned and said to Muzhou, "I did what you kindly told me but each time I asked my question, the master hit me. I simply don't understand! It appears I'm unable to grasp the profound meaning of all this and so I'll be on my way." (Zen practitioners: Does this sound familiar?) Muzhou, who really was playing a fine supportive teaching role, then said, "Well, monk, if you must, you must, but first make sure you say goodbye to the master." Linji bowed and, as he went to gather his belongings, Muzhou ran quickly to Huangbo's quarters. "Master," he said, "that young man who questioned you three times is someone special. He'll shape up to be a fine teacher one day. Please help him." So when Linji came to say goodbye, Huangbo said, "Young monk, you mustn't think of leaving! Go over to my Dharma brother Dayu's place by the rapids in Gao'an. He'll explain things to you." Probably relieved that he didn't get another blow, Linji bowed and did as he was told.

He set off on foot to the monastery of Master Gao'an Dayu (J. Koan Daigu), thinking, perhaps, as he walked, "Finally someone will explain what's going on." After finding out that Linji had come from Huangbo's, Dayu asked him whether Huangbo had had any teaching words for him when he had gone in for the interview. Linji once again told his story about asking the question three times, and of each time being struck. "I don't know what I did wrong," he said dejectedly. At this Dayu sighed. "That poor Huangbo. What a kind grandmother he is. Wearing himself out, striking you, and you come here asking whether you did anything wrong or not!" At which moment Linji awakened. The "meaning" of the Buddha's teaching is just this (*blow*), just this (*blow*), just this (*blow*). There is no meaning. There is only "just this"—and *that* is the meaning.

Linji got it. Simple!—and he said so: "Well, Huangbo's teaching wasn't so hard after all!" (Quite a dramatic change from the timid fellow of before.) Dayu grabbed him. "You little bed-wetting fellow! One minute saying you did something wrong, the next saying there's nothing hard about the Dharma! Tell me, what truth have you learned? What is it that you have realized?" Upon which Linji punched Dayu three times in the ribs. "Go back to Huangbo's," said Dayu, probably laughing heartily. "He's your teacher."

So an awakened and bruised Linji returned. He went to the master and thanked Huangbo for his "motherly kindness." "What did Dayu teach you?" asked Huangbo. When Linji reported what had happened, he bellowed, "Oh, if only I could get my hands on Dayu. I'd give him a big wallop!" "Hey," said Linji, "I'll give you the wallop right now." And he gave Huangbo a big smack. "Attendant!" the master hollered, "Get this crazy man out of here and take him to the monks' hall." Linji was on his way.

Now, Huangbo was saying, *now* your Zen really begins. You've let go of trying to find out the meaning of the Buddha Way. You've let go of the rules and the teachings. You've stopped being frustrated and sorry for yourself and wanting to walk out because you don't understand. You stopped and listened, with a still mind, and didn't get all tied up in knots about not being good enough. You just stopped. And with your exemplary years of discipline, structure, and dedication as a base, with your meticulous attention to detail, you finally heard the meaning of Zen Buddhism come forth. *Slap! Poke!* No meaning! Just this! Whatever is in front of you. So now, go to the monks' hall and practice being present to your life, alive and fresh to every moment. And that is what Linji did. He was liberated.

What mind clutter stands in the way of your receiving each moment as it arises? And what are you going to do about it? That is the encouragement of this fabulous teaching.

NO MENTION IS MADE in the records of Linji being personally affected by the severe persecutions directed against Buddhism at this time—persecutions that were to have a lasting impact on the future of Buddhism in China. In 845, Emperor Wuzong, an ardent Taoist who felt Buddhism was a growing threat to his power, gave orders for the elimination of many Buddhist enclaves. His harsh orders were not only of a religious nature but were also aimed at diminishing the growing economic and political muscle of Buddhist monasteries that up till then had been tax-exempt and growing in power. Monasteries and temples were destroyed or closed, and monks and nuns placed back on the tax rolls. The persecutions were severe though short-lived because Wuzong died the following year and his successor, Emperor Xuanzong, relaxed the harsh measures somewhat, even allowing some temples to be rebuilt. Establishment Buddhism survived, but it never regained its former strength, "suffering" as the scholar Heinrich Dumoulin writes, "wounds that would leave it permanently crippled [in China]."

Zen, however, not only survived but thrived. It was affected the least probably because its temples and monasteries were far from urban centers, and its teachers were not politically inclined. However, there may have been other reasons. Perhaps it survived because its teaching focused on detachment from the world of gain, power, identity, and ego. Perhaps it survived because of the integrity of those Zen masters in the far-off temples who insisted that this teaching be lived out. Whatever the reason, Zen became established during the dreadful years of the An Lushan rebellion one hundred years earlier; it thrived during the persecutions of 845.

During this period Linji spent time with both Huangbo and Dayu. The record tells us that at Huangbo's monastery he worked the fields with the other monks (manual labor now being a major part of the new monastic order) and participated in a monastic life that was highly structured. He may also have been Huangbo's right-hand man: at one point, the record tells us, he delivered a letter from Huangbo to another monastery. All this is important to note for our practice today because it reinforces the fact that Linji's later teaching, which scandalized so many, was based on highly developed discipline, on the ability to work with others, and on deep respect for his teacher—characteristics often overlooked when one thinks of Linji's radical disregard for authority of any kind.

Zen practitioners would do well to note that it takes a person grounded in such disciplines and egoless respect to "kill" authority. A person thus awakened clearly sees that "authority" is only an idea with potentially dangerous consequences. For if one succumbs to another's authority at one's own expense, or thinks oneself superior at another's expense, one continues living in the world of duality, the world of opposition, thus totally missing the truth that there is no "other," and that "other" and "me" are ideas imposed on the Oneness that just is. Linji smacked his teachers and they received the blows because both parties had awakened to the truth of not-two, had shed their ideas of "teacher" and "student," shed their ideas of "me" and "you." They "disappeared," if you will, and simply reveled in the flow of the "just this." But, utterly important to note, they were awakened. And they had awakened through the solid foundation of discipline, structure, and respect for "other."

Nowhere is this "disappearance of self" better expressed than in Linji's famous teaching of "the true man of no rank."

"Attention!" Linji addressed the assembly: "There is a true person of no rank... always leaving and entering the gates of your face. You beginners who have not witnessed [this person of no rank]: Look! Look!"

This expression "true person of no rank" comes up only once in the Linji-lu but the phrase and teaching took hold, and became koan 38 in *The Book of Equanimity*. This person of no rank is a person with no status, no identified place in society—a marginal figure, one who doesn't count, doesn't really exist. A nobody. To realize just who this nobody is, this person of no rank, always coming and going, hearing and responding, living and dying in each moment of life, we practice stilling our discriminating mind through *zazen*. In addition, we undertake the practice of no ranking—no labeling, no judging, no comparing—in daily life. This requires diligence, for we tend to constantly rank. And that is why the teaching begins with "Attention!" Be awake! Be aware every time you rank, judge, label yourself, others, situations, your practice, your work, your life—whatever. Catch it. Notice it. Step back from that identity label, that judging word, that comparing perception. Step back and be with what's left—the true person of no rank.

Certainly we need to have identities and to discriminate in order to live in the world, and we must make distinctions. They are, after all, the basis of the Buddha's Eightfold Path: right thought, right intent, right speech, right action, right livelihood, right effort, right mindfulness, and right meditation. These all assume a "not right": a not-right thought, a not-right intent, and so forth. Indeed, Linji railed at teachers who didn't make distinctions, calling them a "bunch of baldheads who...love clear weather, love it when it rains, love this lamp or that pillar. Teachers like that are nothing but wild fox spirits, goblins." So we can, indeed must, make distinctions, as long as we don't cling to them, as long as the distinctions are made by the person of no rank. And what is a life of no ranking? Linji says in another passage, "In the eye it's called seeing. In the ear it's called hearing. In the nose it smells odors. In the mouth it holds conversation. In the hand it grasps and seizes. In the feet it runs and carries." It is, in other words, your ordinary human life. This was to become Linji's foundational teaching.

AFTER RECEIVING the seal of transmission from Huangbo, Linji traveled across China visiting other masters—one of whom, Deshan Xuanjian (J. Tokusan Senkan), we will meet in a later chapter. He finally settled down in northern China in the city of Zhenzhou where, as the pagoda inscription tells us, "he became the head of a small monastery overlooking the Hu-t'o River...The name Lin-chi, which means 'overlooking the ford,' derives from the location of the temple." It is here that Linji's teaching and teaching style came alive. And it was honesty and deep devotion to the Dharma that drove him.

Zen practitioners in the middle of the ninth century seem to have faced many of the same obstacles Zen practitioners do today. They kept looking for "something other," seeking to gain "something else"; they relied too much on books and the words of teachers; they thought that Zen was a dropping off into some kind of nonworldly space, cut off from daily living in an attempt to become enlightened. It was these people that Linji thundered at—as he thunders at us: "I tell you, there's no Buddha, no Dharma, no practice, no enlightenment. Yet you go off like this on side roads, trying to find something. Blind fools! Will you put another head on top of the one you have? What is it you lack?"

"Followers of the Way," Linji railed, "you take the words that come out of the mouths of a bunch of old teachers to be a description of the true Way. You think, 'This is a most wonderful teacher and friend. I have only the mind of a common mortal, I would never dare try to fathom such venerable-ness.' Blind idiots! You go through life...betraying your own two eyes."

"Followers of the Way," he continued, "if you want to get the kind of understanding that accords with the Dharma, never be misled by others. Whether you're facing inward or facing outward, whatever you meet up with, just kill it! If you meet a buddha, kill the buddha. If you meet a patriarch, kill the patriarch...If you meet your parents, kill your parents...Then, for the first time you will gain emancipation, will not be entangled with things, will pass freely anywhere you wish to go."

Linji certainly called a spade a spade, with passion and shocking tactics. His blunt disregard for authority and structure surely must have shocked many back then and perhaps still does today. But to those who today would accuse him of setting himself up as being beyond authority, he says: "I don't have a particle of Dharma to give to anyone." To those who would accuse him of doing away with the need for a teacher, he says, "You should go around hunting for a teacher. Don't just drift along, always trying to take the easy way." To those who would accuse him of doing away with formal teaching, the dialectical formula of "The Four Propositions," as laid out in Section 10 of the Linji-lu, would be his answer. And to those who would accuse him of doing away with meditation, the record shows glimpses of a functioning meditation hall, which would have been such a given in the strict monastic rule of Baizhang that it would have never needed to be addressed in the record. Does all this contradict his teaching to cease practice and give up study and forget about meditation and teachers? Of course! Zen teaching is a paradox.

The sole purpose of Linji's blunt words was to jolt practitioners into seeing the truth, and in this he proved that he was a deeply compassionate man. This giant of a teacher is like a man on the side of a surging river that is carrying people toward a dangerous waterfall. He sees innumerable ropes dangling down from trees and he's desperately doing all he can to help them see these many ropes that can free them from the waters. But they don't see the ropes, for they are looking for boats or big rocks or other things in the water to cling to. They don't look further than their limited ideas of what can save them; they look for what they think they should be looking for and don't see the hanging ropes. And there is Linji on the shore, shouting, "Look! Look! Wake up! Grab the ropes! They are your very life! Don't look for something else! The Way is right in front of you. Can't you see?" Probably most of them could not see, as we so often cannot, because their minds, like ours, were so cluttered with their ideas of Zen, ideas of holiness, ideas of enlightenment and Buddha and Dharma. They could not see, as we so often cannot see. "Yet, you must see," Linji passionately urges. "You must see the moment as it is—honestly. See yourself as you are—honestly. See others as they are—honestly. See life as it is—honestly. This is the Way."

How do we do this? We sit. We practice stilling the ego-mind, creator of ideas, expectations, and obligations. We practice earnestly, as Linji did, probing and polishing, not striving to achieve, not striving to know something, not striving to get somewhere, not striving to become someone; striving, rather, to realize nothing. "Doing nothing," he called it, simply surrendering to each moment, allowing each moment to lead us and teach us as it unfolds, trusting the structure and form of "just this" to hold us in the "just now." For it is only in the strictest of disciplines, such as Linji had imposed upon himself in his formative years and imposed on those who practiced with him, that one can trust oneself to let go into the constantly changing and unfolding not-knowing of one's life.

Linji taught not only the monks who came to his monastery but also lay people interested in awakening through the way of Chan. These were ordinary people in whose homes he was welcomed for meals. He was also welcomed into the homes of those in power, which may account for the fact that, when fighting forced Linji to abandon his temple overlooking the ford (these were the years when the Tang dynasty was deteriorating and unrest was gripping much of the land), "Grand Commandant Mei Chun-ho gave up his own house within the city walls and turned it into a temple, hanging up the Linji plaque there and inviting the master to take up residence." For a while he went south, although we do not know why, but eventually he returned north of the Yangtze and settled in the temple of his Dharma heir Xinghua Cunjiang (J. Koke Sonsho), who took care of him in his final years.

Linji died in 867. His deathbed exchange with another Dharma heir, Sangshen Huiran (J. Sansho Enen), as set down in koan 13 of *The Book of Equanimity*, reveals that his penetrating insight into the heart of reality would live on. "Don't let my True Dharma Eye be extinguished," he exhorted Sangshen. "How could I let it be extinguished?" asked the disciple. "If, after I have passed away, someone asks you about it, how will you reply?" Linji asked. Sangshen gave a shout. "Who would have thought," said Linji, "that my True Dharma Eye would be extinguished on reaching this blind donkey?" A blind donkey, as Roshi Shishin Wick tells us in his commentary on this koan, is "a liberated person who maintains the heart of not-knowing, not seeing." He goes on to say, "How could you extinguish something that's unborn and undying?"

Linji was fifty-seven when he died. We don't know the cause of his relatively early death. Perhaps he had given his all and could give no more. Perhaps his 100 percent passion for seeking to have his fellow human travelers, including you and me, see those ropes hanging down in the surging river finally gave out.

But the ropes are still there for us, if only we can stop looking for boulders and rafts.

7. ZHAOZHOU

J. JOSHU; 778–897

GO HAVE SOME TEA

ONE DAY, sometime between 837 and 857, an elderly monk named Congshen stopped by the monastery of a Zen master for an interview. The master was just then washing his feet in a bucket in the courtyard. Congshen, thirty years older than the master, paid his respects and then asked a question familiar to many Zen practitioners today: "What is the meaning of Bodhidharma's coming from the west?" The master replied, "As it now happens, I'm washing my feet." Congshen came closer and made as if listening. "All right, I'll have to throw out a second ladle of dirty water," said the master. Congshen turned and left. The interview was over. Congshen had demonstrated his Zen eye. They both had. Surely the master must have smiled as he dried his feet.

The players in this little monastic drama were none other than Master Linji Yixuan and Zhaozhou Congshen (J. Joshu Jushin). The latter would become known as one of the greatest teachers of Zen's Golden Age but at this time was known only as Congshen. He was in his sixties or seventies, had experienced his breakthrough enlightenment experience over forty years before, and was now on a twenty-year pilgrimage to deepen his Zen insight. In the monastery courtyard he had met his peer.

Congshen was testing Linji (a favorite sport of Zen teachers at the time). "What is the meaning of Zen?" he was essentially asking. "Meaning? Can you show me meaning? Washing my feet—*that* I can show you." "Really? Let me see." (As if Congshen didn't know.) "Well,

I suppose I'll have to show you again." End of meeting. Match draw. Who was interviewing whom?

"Meaning" is an idea. Zen does not subscribe to ideas, only to "just this" experience. But *we* subscribe to meaning, don't we? We are constantly asking, "What is the meaning of—?" Then we get entangled in the answers, either someone else's or our own. Why get entangled, these two awakened people ask us. Just wash your feet. Or, as Zhaozhou later said to a traveling monk who came to him seeking instruction, "Have you had your breakfast?" "Yes." Pause. The monk missed the instruction. "Well, go and wash your bowl," said Zhaozhou, kindly offering the instruction again. The record states that then "the monk had some realization." What did he realize? That the primary instruction was to be present to *this* moment, *this* task. Stop looking for "Zen." Pay attention!

ZHAOZHOU WAS BORN in 778, ten years before Mazu's passing and twelve years before Shitou's, in a village in northern China. Being very interested in Buddhist teachings, he entered a monastery at an early age and received ordination as a novice monk while still in his mid teens. Sensing, however, that this was not quite the right place for him, he followed his instincts, left the monastery before full ordination, and set out to find his true teacher. Here on display is Zhaozhou's confidence in his own voice at a very early age, a time of life usually filled with confusion and dependence on outer sources of wisdom and teaching. Not so with Zhaozhou. Although he could not articulate what he was looking for, he intuited that it was not to be found in this monastic setting. Zhaozhou provides an encouraging model for practitioners today: the deepest parts of ourselves must be listened to, trusted, and acted upon, not just while practicing *zazen* on the cushion but during all parts of one's life. Timidity and hesitation because of a mindset that says, "who are you to know anything about such and such?" must always be examined. Is it a call to learn more from someone else, or is it a call to be bold, take risks, face fears, and trust in oneself? For Zhaozhou it was the latter, and so, as a young man of seventeen, facing his fears, he set out to find a teacher who fit.

It turns out that he felt not only that his old monastery was not the place for him. Monasteries in general were not for him, for the teacher he found did not live in a monastery but in relative seclusion on Mount Nanquan, from which the teacher had taken his name. Nanquan Puyuan (J. Nansen Fugan) was one of the two most influential successors of the prolific Zen master Mazu, the other being Baizhang. Unlike Baizhang, who not only chose the monastic path but also developed new guidelines for monastic living and discipline, Nanquan chose a mostly secluded life, living on his mountain for thirty years after receiving Dharma transmission at age forty-eight.

A year after Nanquan's arrival there, Zhaozhou appeared on his doorstep one early spring day. History does not tell us how Zhaozhou found Nanquan but find him he did, and he remained with him until Nanquan's death thirty-four years later. It is one of the most enduring teacher-student relationships in all of Zen history. Here is a description of their meeting, taken from the Recorded Teachings of Zen Master Zhaozhou or the Chao-chou Chan Shih Yu-lu, written by one of Zhaozhou's disciples in the tenth century.

Nanquan is sitting in his room. Zhaozhou enters.

"Where have you come from?"

"From Shuixiang [which means 'the temple of the standing image']."

"Then did you see the standing image [of the Buddha] there?"

"No, I don't see a standing image. I see a reclining Tathagata [one of the names for a buddha or awakened person]."

"Are you a novice with a master or a novice without a master?"

"A novice with a master."

"Where is your master?"

"In spite of the intense cold of early spring, I dare say your honorable body is enjoying good health."

One can imagine Nanquan nodding. His student had arrived.

This method of asking a newly arrived seeker "Where are you from?" was a common way for Zen masters to discern a student's insight. Here is how it might be stated in a modern context: "Where are you from?" "I'm from Chicago." "Did you feel the wind blowing in Chicago?" "I feel no wind but I smell the incense in this room."

Do you see? What Chicago? What Shuixiang? What buddha statue? Just a buddha sitting in front of me. For the Zen, nondualistic eye, there is no Shuixiang, there is no buddha statue, there is no Chicago. These are mental concepts; they do not exist as separate entities somewhere else—they are here, for there is only "just this," "just here." Young Zhaozhou did not get caught in the mental concepts of "back there"—and neither must we. No thoughts about the past, no thoughts about the future, no thoughts about over there, no conceptual idea of "Chicago"— only "just this," here and now. The "Chicago" I left yesterday is not where I am today. This is why we must cultivate awareness and attentiveness to what is in front of us right now—a cultivation that brings freedom from the burdens of a past that no longer exists and a future that has not happened. But how do we do it? Here is unambiguous advice from Zhaozhou in his later years. A monk asked him, "What is the practice hall?" Zhaozhou said, "From the practice hall you have come, from the practice hall you will go. Everything [everywhere] is the practice hall. There is no other place." There is no other time. There is only the continual flow of practicing awareness of what is in front of us.

And this is why Zen is so structured. It is not structured because it is Chinese or Japanese or Korean, or because of the controlling tendencies of a teacher or the tradition of the process. It is structured because structures provide compassionate, moment-to-moment footholds that ground us in the present and allow less possibility of slippage into the ego-mind's illusions. Structures and disciplines are on our side, no matter how much we rebel against them, and we ignore them at our peril. That is why we must practice until the day we draw our last breath, practice the moment-to-moment mindfulness to whatever is right here. We realize the truth only through practice.

Zhaozhou at a later time: "A monk asked, 'Men of today are honored because of their wealth. For what is a sangha member honored?' The master said, 'Shut your mouth right now.' The monk said, 'If I shut my mouth, do I have it or not?' The master said, 'If you don't shut your mouth, how will you realize it?'" If you don't shut your mouth, how will you realize it? Books, discussions, talk—all pull us into the world of conceptual thinking. That is why Zen so strongly encourages not only a period of meditation in the morning and the evening but also extended periods of practice—for a day, three or four days, a week, or longer. These extended retreats, or *sesshin* as they are called in Japanese, offer us a chance to distance ourselves from our ever-present ego-mind interpretations, concepts, judgments, and memories for much longer periods of time, something that is not possible when, after a half hour or so of morning sitting, we are right back in the mix of our hectic, unfocused lives.

So the young Zhaozhou was welcomed as Nanquan's student. There may have been a few others, either then or in the coming months and years, forming a small meditating community in that mountain residence, a community practicing together, learning from the master, training in the ways of Zen. One can imagine an earnest and serious group of practitioners, none more serious than Zhaozhou. He was a natural, and much of the teaching must have come easily to him, but, in spite of his innate gifts, in that initial interview he had not yet penetrated deeply enough into the mystery of the Way. This was to change in a face-to-face meeting he had with Nanquan at some later point (we don't know when) in his training. It is a famous exchange, the first one in *The Recorded Sayings of Zen Master Joshu* as well as koan 19 in *The Gateless Gate*, translated here by the late Koun Yamada Roshi:

"What is the Way?" Joshu earnestly asked Nansen.
Nansen answered, "The ordinary mind is the Way."
Joshu asked, "Should I direct myself toward it or not?"
Nansen said, "If you try to turn toward it, you go against it."
Joshu asked, "If I do not try to turn toward it, how can I know that it is the Way?"
Nansen answered, "The Way does not belong to knowing or not-knowing. Knowing is delusion; not-knowing is a blank

consciousness. When you have really reached the true Way beyond all doubt, you will find it as vast and boundless as the great empty firmament. How can it be talked about on the level of [being the] right or wrong [Way]?"

At these words, Zhaozhou was suddenly enlightened. He realized that you can't *talk about* the Way, you can't *turn toward* the Way, you can't *know* the Way. If you could talk about it, turn toward it, or know about it, it would be outside of you—something else. This is dualistic thinking. The Way is not outside of you. It is you! Your ordinary, everyday mind: you. So you must stop seeking the Way outside of yourself and pay full attention to this moment with a nonseeking, nondiscriminating, nonseparating mind. It is that simple. But do we trust such teaching? Or does our discriminating, need-to-know mind still need to *know*? Is it caught up in "right and wrong"? Until this discriminating mind is still, realization of the truth cannot arise. When it is still, it is simple. No problem. "Just this." "Have you had your breakfast? Then go and wash your bowl and don't look for anything extra." Zen is not about adding anything, it is about subtracting everything.

Zhaozhou had realized the truth. The Way is not outside of me—it *is* me. He taught this simple message, ever more simply, for the rest of his life. *The Recorded Sayings of Zen Master Joshu* tells us that an earnest monk once asked him the same question, "What is the Way?" "It's just outside the fence," said Zhaozhou (surely smiling). "But I'm asking about the Great Way," said the monk. "Oh, the *great* way! Well, that's different! The great way leads to the capital." Isn't that a delightful expression of profound teaching? What "Great Way"? All ideas are programmed into your mind. Go to the meditation hall and sit, he might have then told the monk. Stop asking questions that can't be answered. Go to the meditation hall and sit and you will realize (*realize*, not *know*) the Great Way without any doubt.

This direct and simple teaching, found in the more than five hundred recorded sayings of this master, reflects again how the teaching and expression of the Dharma develops from generation to generation. Zhaozhou's respect for his teacher knew no bounds, as we shall see, but he did not copy his teacher. When asked the same question he himself had asked as a novice monk, he did not speak of "ordinary mind"; he spoke *as* ordinary mind. What is the Way? The way is outside the fence. The way, obviously, *is* outside the fence. Don't look for any other way. Go and wash your bowl. Simplification, directness, emptiness—all expressed in Zhaozhou's most famous teaching of *Mu*, or "not," the basis of the first koan in the *The Gateless Gate*. "Does a dog have buddha nature?" a monk asked. "*Mu*," was the answer. "Not."

IN HIS LATE TEENS or early twenties, Zhaozhou (still known as Congshen) awakened to the truth. So what did he do? Go off to be a hermit? Go off on pilgrimage to learn more? Go off to found his own community? No, he stayed exactly where he was. He stayed with his teacher, Nanquan (now in his early fifties), until Nanquan's death at the age of eighty-seven, when Zhaozhou was fifty-six years old. This choice—and it surely must have been a choice—seems to me to be one of the most remarkable things about this remarkable man. He was content to live out possibly the rest of his life (how did he know he was going to outlive his teacher?), and certainly the prime of his life, in relative obscurity on a mountain. He was content to walk the talk and actually *live* ordinary mind at its most ordinary level. He was content to disappear. Could it be that this choice, the choice to disappear, is what eventually made him the supreme teacher that he became? How paradoxical. The Tao te Ching says it best in this translation by Stephen Mitchell:

> The master, by residing in the Tao [the Way],
> sets an example for all beings.
> Because he doesn't display himself,
> people can see his light.
> Because he has nothing to prove,
> people can trust his words.
> Because he doesn't know who he is,
> people recognize themselves in him.
> Because he has no goal in mind,
> everything he does succeeds.

This is a perfect description of Zhaozhou and a great model and challenge for us. Do *we* walk the talk, or is our insight limited to the zendo while our ego-centered lives continue unabated outside? We live in an age where everybody wants his and her fifteen minutes of fame. We all have egos, and our ego-mind always wants to be special, wants to stand out, wants to be noticed, wants to be different. (This applies equally when ego-mind tries *not* to be noticed, when it doesn't speak out and hides in the back of the room—often a plea to "notice me.") This ego-centered drive is part of our ignorance. We must get to know this part of ourselves and attend to it with courage. How do we do this? As always, by practicing the stilling of that ego-centered mind through zazen.

So Zhaozhou stayed with his teacher, content to be the disciple, content to live out moment after succeeding moment in the mountain community. However, by 825 Nanquan's reputation as a gifted teacher had spread, and he was eventually persuaded by the powerful provincial governor, Lu Geng, who became his patron and later his devoted student, to leave the isolation of the mountain so that more people could be exposed to his teaching. Zhaozhou followed Nanquan and for the next ten years they served the newly formed monastic community that the governor had helped establish. Many people came, the Recorded Teachings tell us, and the monastic life there was captured in some recorded exchanges: the monks argue and there is a monastery cat (the monks and this cat being the basis of koan 14 in *The Gateless Gate*); Nanquan tends a garden; Zhaozhou tends fires and draws water from the well; there is a bathing area; Nanquan wields the stick like his teacher, Mazu; the governor comes to pay his respects; and, through it all, Nanquan and Zhaozhou teach as a team. It was, indeed, an enduring teacher-student relationship.

In 835, Nanquan was eighty-seven years old. One day he became ill and said to his monks, "The star's light is dim, but eternal. Don't say that I'm coming or going." When he had finished speaking, he died. The monks entered into a three-year period of mourning, a tribute to the respect in which Nanquan was held. There is no record of what happened during these three years, so it is not possible to know whether or not Zhaozhou took over the leadership of the monastery, but it seems unlikely, for at the end of the three years he left. He was sixty years old.

And now we come to another significant choice Zhaozhou made after his awakening—the first being to remain with his teacher until his death. He decided to set out on a pilgrimage, an unusual decision. After all, he was at an age when people usually settle down rather than begin traveling. And he could have taken over the leadership of the monastic community and made a name for himself; the influential governor would surely have supported him, and his reputation would have been secure. No, Zhaozhou, the iconoclast, carrying his own water jug and staff, set out on a pilgrimage to cultivate his practice further, vowing to learn from anyone who could teach him, even if it was a young child, and to instruct anyone who needed him, even if it was an elder (elders were deeply respected in Chinese society as being the wisest ones). One would be hard pressed to find a better example of open awareness than this. When one has disappeared—no ego, no self—don't teaching and learning become one? When I need to learn, I learn, when I need to teach, I teach. There is a wonderful story told about Roshi Hugo Enomiya LaSalle and the famous twentieth-century Zen master Koun Yamada Roshi, who was his teacher. When LaSalle Roshi was eighty and a well-known teacher in his own right, Yamada Roshi told him that he, LaSalle, still had something to learn. So LaSalle closed down his zendo and went back to just sitting, waiting in line, along with everyone else, for his dokusan interviews.

Pilgrimage—seeking out Zen masters across China—could not have been easy for anyone, much less a sixty-year-old. Zhaozhou walked, as did all other monks on pilgrimage, on earthen roads and across planks in the mountains and rocks in the streams. He would have covered about seventeen miles a day at best and probably often had to sleep by the roadside, as inns and monasteries that welcomed travelers must have been few and far between. We think of China as a hugely populated country but recall that after the An Lushan rebellion the population had dropped to fifteen million, with most people living in cities. It must have been desolate at times and dangerous as well, since bandits roamed the countryside and food was probably scarce—begged for or picked from the roadside. Yes, to go on pilgrimage was no picnic, yet Zhaozhou journeyed like this for twenty years until he was eighty years old, curious, alive, responsive. Linji, as mentioned at the beginning of this chapter, was only one of the many renowned Zen teachers he visited. The few interchanges between Zhaozhou and his peers that were recorded reveal a keen Zen eye, nimble wit, and always skillful teaching.

Along the way he must have witnessed many signs of a collapsing empire, for by now the Tang dynasty was truly in its downward spiral. In 845, the Buddhist persecutions under Emperor Wuzong had probably affected some of the monasteries Zhaozhou visited, and the feudal warfare that enveloped the land as the Tang emperors became weaker and weaker surely affected general living conditions throughout the country. Whether he stopped because of this or other reasons, Zhaozhou ended his travels in the year 858. He was back in northern China, which he had left so many years ago, and he took up residence in a run-down old temple in the province of Zhaozhou. And that is how Congshen became Master Zhaozhou of Guanyin (the Bodhisattva of Compassion) Temple, where he lived and taught for the next forty years. Yes, Zhaozhou died when he was 120. The temple (though not its original building, of course) welcomes visitors to this day and is now known as Pailin Temple.

According to the record, living conditions in the temple were awful. The monks' hall had no walls on two sides, there was little food for the midday meal, robes were tattered, donkeys ate the weeds out front, rats ran around, and even the master's chair was broken—and he refused to have it fixed. Money was scarce, but never once in his forty years of residence did Zhaozhou send out a letter asking for support. How amazing! Even when support was offered by various officials who called on him, he refused to take it. What does this teach us about our own need for comforts, our need for things and possessions, our need to make an appearance and live out an image, our need to always look for something else? What does this teach us about the ensuing frustration, anxiety, and restlessness when these needs are not met? "The true Way is without difficulty," Zhaozhou once said, "just refrain from picking and choosing," echoing the singular teaching of the third ancestor, Master Sengcan.

Although it is difficult to imagine how such an old man—a centenarian—survived under these conditions, survive he did. Maybe he even thrived. He taught directly, plainly, simply, and to the point. After all, teaching can't be simpler than *Mu*—"not"—in describing what the Heart Sutra calls the "emptiness of the five human conditions." Because he so lived out this emptiness, he was not caught by the mind's delusions and spins and could respond immediately and brilliantly to any question. The limited confines of his ego-mind had pretty much disappeared, and he could not be caught in its trap. A monk once asked him, "I am chaotically adrift and drowning. How can I get out of it?" We today might ask, "Should I go to a therapist? Should I go on vacation? Should I pray? Should I have a drink? Should I do yoga? How can I get out of it?" Zhaozhou just sat motionless. The monk cried out, "I'm asking you sincerely!" Please help me! "Where are you adrift and drowning?" replied the master.

As we have seen, Zhaozhou's teaching also sprang from the circumstances of an ordinary life, and many students caught in lofty ideas about "Zen" were quickly brought back to reality in the most grandmotherly of ways. It was said that he made tea an essential part of Zen, and his favorite reply to a question was "go have some tea." And he meant it. Here is one example: Two new arrivals came to the front door. To the first arrival, he said, "Have you been here before?" "No, I haven't." "Go have some tea." To the second arrival, he said, "Have you been here before?" "Yes, I have." "Go have some tea." The head monk overheard and asked, "Why did you tell each of them to do the same thing?" They are different and should be treated differently, he implied. "Head monk!" Zhaozhou exclaimed. "Yes." "Go have some tea." It is no wonder that so many flocked to him. Wouldn't you?

Among those who were drawn to Zhaozhou were women—nuns as well as laity. The half-dozen or so encounters between him and women related in *The Recorded Sayings of Zen Master Joshu* (quite a goodly number, given that women were so rarely mentioned as having any role to play in the lives of the ancestors), reveal relationships that were on a peer level and surprisingly intimate. In one exchange with an old woman carrying bamboo shoots, he asked the woman where she was taking them. When she said "to Zhaozhou," the master asked her what she would do when she saw Zhaozhou. The old woman promptly slapped him, concluding a real peer-to-peer exchange. One can imagine Zhaozhou having a hearty laugh. On another occasion, a nun asked, "What is the deeply secret mind?" The master squeezed her hand. The nun said, "Do you still have that in you?" The master said, "It is you who have it." Unafraid of intimacy, this insightful man, so free in the Dharma, expresses "the deeply secret mind" in a totally spontaneous and unselfconscious way. No wonder many flocked to him.

The large numbers were due not only to his teaching but to two other factors related to his environs. The city of Zhaozhou was a resting place for pilgrims visiting the two hundred or so monasteries (some of which stand to this day) on the nearby sacred mountain of Wutai. Many of these pilgrims surely stopped at Guanyin Temple and some may have even stopped by the tea stand of an old woman at the base of the mountain who, along with Zhaozhou, plays a leading role in koan 31 of *The Gateless Gate*. The city was also a tourist attraction of sorts because of its famous bridge, built in the year 600 and still the oldest stone-arch bridge in the world. Zen koan students will recognize this bridge as the subject of koan 52 in *The Blue Cliff Record* (although, strangely, in the koan it is not described as an arched structure but as stepping-stones). The city of Zhaozhou was a busy place, and many of its residents and visitors, including provincial governors and various other officials, came to speak with its famous Zen master.

IN THIS FASHION, Zhaozhou lived the last third of his life, forty years. One would think that such a rich teaching legacy would produce a large number of Dharma heirs and perhaps a Zhaozhou school of Zen. This was not the case. He left few successors, his line ran out rather quickly, and his name is not mentioned in any Zen lineage. Suggested theories as to why this was so include the difficult living conditions in the temple, societal unrest, the subtlety of Zhaozhou's teaching, the endless flow of visitors, and his physical condition (how much could a hundred-year-old man do?), but whatever the reason, one wonders whether it was even important to him. In the same way, Mozart, as one modern conductor has said, did not write for posterity, he "wrote for Saturday [night]." Naturals have a way of not being concerned about being remembered.

In spite of the fact that there was no Zhaozhou school of Zen, 525 anecdotes about Zhaozhou appear in the Recorded Teachings, and his brilliant, often witty, exchanges and simple, pointed teachings appear nineteen times in *The Gateless Gate* and *The Blue Cliff Record*, second only to twenty-three teachings by Master Yunmen (who had an unfair advantage because his Dharma great-grandson was the editor of *The Blue Cliff Record*).

In the year 897, Zhaozhou died. Before passing away, he asked that his teaching stick be sent to the governor of the province with the words, "I have not finished using this in my lifetime." After his death, the record tells us that monks and lay people numbering in the thousands came out, and that "sounds of lamentation shook the meadows and fields."

How would Zhaozhou want us to remember him? Surely there can be only one answer. "Go have some tea."

8. DONGSHAN

J. TOZAN; 807–869

AVOID SEEKING ELSEWHERE

IF ONE WERE to look down on ninth-century China from a time-traveling spaceship with the capability of locating brilliant Zen masters, its sensors would certainly light up. There were so many of them. The origins of Zen that had been brought from India by Bodhidharma, that had found focus through Huineng and been shaped by Mazu and Shitou in the previous two centuries, had by now flowered into the golden years of Chan. Baizhang was still alive at the dawn of this century, as was his successor, Huangbo, who, along with *his* successor, Linji, both taught vigorously till midcentury. Nanquan and Guishan, both directly connected to Mazu, lived and taught the Dharma during this time, as did Deshan and Xuefeng, whom we have yet to meet. Zhaozhou, of course, was alive, for his life spanned almost the entire century. And these were just the giants. What a time to be born a seeker—exactly the time when Dongshan Liangjie (J. Tozan Ryokai), founder of the Caodong (J. Soto) school of Zen (flourishing to this day), entered the scene.

Dongshan was born in 807 in far eastern China, in modern Zhejiang Province, and from a very early age he was drawn to Buddhism, which he wanted to understand. During his studies as a young boy, he queried his Buddhist teacher about his puzzlement regarding the words "no eye, ear, nose, tongue, body, mind" in the Heart Sutra, when, as he said, he clearly had these attributes. The teacher (probably a Vinaya master) responded by advising him to study the Chan way. So Dongshan went to study with Zen Master Limo on Mount Wuxie and eventually received ordination as a monk on Mount Song, famous as the location of Bodhidharma's cave. He was then about twenty years old.

"I have eyes, ears, a nose, and so on. So why does the sutra say there is none?" Is this not the same question that arises for today's Zen inquirer upon first sight of these lines in the Heart Sutra? To say there are no eyes or ears is absurd, so why does the Great Heart of Wisdom Sutra say this is so? Like Dongshan, we want to understand. Well, we can't understand, for the ego-mind cannot answer such questions. Sit, still the discriminating ego-mind, and stop naming what "eyes and ears" see and hear. What happens? Do these things "exist" in that time of not-naming?

After his ordination, Dongshan began the usual monk's pilgrimage to find the right Zen teacher, but his pilgrimage was to last an unusually long time—twenty years. In his quest to find someone who could tell him the answers to the questions that were gnawing at him, he visited numerous masters, many of whom had their temples in the area just south of the Yangtze River in the modern-day provinces of Kiangsi and Hunan. While traveling on foot was difficult for those on a pilgrimage, a number of the major Zen monastic centers that were being established at this time were fairly close to each other, making pilgrimages relatively doable. This concentration of gifted Zen teachers in one area surely played a large part in the exchange not only of students but also of ideas and teaching methods among the teachers themselves. Zen was fluid, being shaped. The Five Schools had not yet been systemized (this was only to happen in the middle of the eleventh century). Seeking out different teachers was encouraged and rivalry between the masters themselves seems to have been nonexistent. All this, as William F. Powell tells us in his introduction to *The Record of Tung-shan*, "gave to the Chan of this period a coherence and momentum that undoubtedly contributed to the significant later influence of this group of masters." What an amazingly creative and vibrant time it must have been for those young monks on pilgrimage.

The first teacher Dongshan approached after his ordination was Nanquan, successor of Mazu and, as we have seen, teacher of Zhaozhou. Both Nanquan and Zhaozhou had by now left their mountain seclusion and located to an urban monastic setting. This makes it quite probable that three of the greatest teachers in Zen history, Nanquan, Zhaozhou and (soon to be) Dongshan, sat together in meditation more than once. Quite a thought! Yet Dongshan does not seem to have spent too much time there and soon left. He left, presumably, because he didn't get the answers and the teaching he wanted or expected, even from an exceptional teacher such as Nanquan—and isn't that just like us? When we don't get the answers we want, the teaching we expect, or when we don't "get it," don't we often go elsewhere, shut down, give up, and stop trying to probe the uncomfortable nature of the Dharma? Dongshan wanted to understand and Nanquan could not help him. Zen is not about understanding, it is about experience, and we have to stay on course until we break through into the experiential understanding of the truth. On the other hand, if a teacher is not right for a practitioner, he or she has to move on and find the right one. Discerning the difference is subtle work, but if the teacher one is leaving has insight into a student, that teacher can greatly assist in the discernment. Who knows? Perhaps it was Nanquan himself who told Dongshan to move on—which is what he did.

Dongshan set off toward Master Guishan's steep mountain monastery, which was far away in Hunan Province. The record does not tell us why he chose to move on to Guishan, whose life and teaching is described in an earlier chapter, but it was probably because Dongshan had heard that the master had the answer to a troubling question he had had for a while—namely whether or not inanimate things possessed buddha nature. This topic had been debated during the formative years of Zen and, although it had been settled by now in favor of all things being able to express the Dharma, it was (and still is) a subject of puzzlement for many. How can inanimate objects teach the Dharma?

After his arrival on Mount Guishan, Dongshan went to meet with the master, telling him about a teaching of the greatly respected national teacher Nanyang Huizhong (J. Nanyo Echu), who appears in koan 17 of *The Gateless Gate*. Nanyang was a Dharma heir of Master Huineng and was the teacher of three Tang emperors, hence his title "national teacher." He taught that nonsentient beings preach the

Dharma, speaking of "wall tile and rubble...constantly expounding it [the Dharma], radiantly expounding it, expounding it without ceasing." When Dongshan confessed that he could not understand this teaching, Guishan said, "This teaching is also taught here at my monastery, but very few people understand it." "Well, I am not one of them," Dongshan replied. "Please, teach me." And that is what Guishan proceeded to do. He held up his *hossu* or flywhisk (the one given to him by his teacher, Baizhang, as a sign of his teaching authority) and asked, "Do you understand?" "I do not," said Dongshan. "Well, I'm afraid the human mouth cannot explain it to you," replied the master, leaving Dongshan's desire for understanding unquenched.

This is a state that is surely familiar to many Zen practitioners today. We want to understand the nonunderstandable and we want to have explained what is not explainable. When something is not explained we can do one of three things: we can stay with the not-knowing of the unexplainable until a way through the gateless gate is realized; we can look elsewhere for some other teacher, some new book, another Dharma talk to explain it; or we can walk away. Just because something is not understandable, just because it can't be explained, does not mean that it is not true. Looking elsewhere, however, is not always a bad thing—as we shall see.

Dongshan decided to look elsewhere. He asked Guishan if there were a teacher who might be able to help him see into the matter, and Guishan referred him to Zen Master Yunyan Tansheng (J. Ungan Donjo), Dharma grandson of Shitou. Master Yunyan was living in a cave on Mount Yunyan—part of a series of connected caves popular with hermits as a place for ascetic practices. Dongshan proceeded there immediately, though it couldn't have been easy to access these mountain caves.

One can't help but be impressed by the determination exhibited by so many of these generative teachers. It offers us an opportunity to examine the question, "Just how much do *I* want to awaken? How determined am I?" It is a foundational question because, without it, one could just meander along, showing up regularly on the meditation mat, feeling a little more calm during the day and being grateful for that but essentially seeing practice as just one of the things one does each day, checking it off when it is done and then getting swallowed up again in the usual hectic pace of life.

Is that what Zen means to you or do you want more? Do *you* want to clarify the Great Matter? Do *you* want to awaken? If so, is the foundational practice of waking up (namely, formal zazen) just one of the daily things you do or is it the most important thing you do? Have you ever asked yourself this question? Might it be helpful to ask now? One can't generate more interest in deepening one's awareness practice if no interest exists, but it is also true that the ego-mind, with its strong conditioning, can keep one at a distance from such deepening. Resistance to meditation practice is subtle and often very strong, and in order to move through it one must make a conscious and often heroic effort. So ask the questions: Is zazen the most important thing I do on any given day? What would it mean for me if it were? What would it take? How much do I want to awaken?

It is clear that Dongshan wanted to awaken. And so he climbed the rough and rocky paths of Mount Yunyan until he reached the master's cave. (How apt that the man who taught the Dharma of nonsentient things should live among rocks.) Upon meeting the master, Dongshan asked who could hear the Dharma expressed by nonsentient beings. Yunyan said, "Nonsentient beings are able to hear it." "Can you hear it?" asked Dongshan. "If I could hear it, then you would not be able to hear it," replied the master. "Why can't I hear it?" asked Dongshan. Yunyan raised his teacher's flywhisk, just as Guishan had. "Can you hear it?" he asked. "No I can't," replied Dongshan. "Well, if you can't hear the Dharma when I teach it, how can you hear it when nonsentient beings teach it?"

What is this exchange about, given the significance it played in the awakening of the founder of a school of Zen still active today? Only that which cannot hear can "hear," because there is nothing to hear. If one could hear it then "it" would be something separate. If one could see it then "it" would be something separate. The National Teacher Nanyang said "wall tile and rubble radiantly expound it [the Dharma] without ceasing" because wall tile and rubble are completely devoid of any interfering "mind." Wall tile and rubble and all nonsentient beings simply *are.* (It is instructive that *The Record of Tung-shan* speaks of nonsentient "beings" and not "things.") This is their radiance and we would do well to pay heed, for is not our right effort to also simply be? The Dharma of nonsentient beings is indeed a profound Dharma and the very muteness of rocks, rubble, trees, and grasses as they express their ineffable nature is a model for us all. It is more than probable that Zen's known connection to rocks, sand, and driftwood, to simple objects simply displayed, to flowers and dry gardens, arises in part from this profound Dharma of nonsentient beings. It was a Dharma that was supported by the nature-based, Chinese Tao te Ching and one that found a deep connection to the Shinto religion when Chan moved to Japan. For us, it is a Dharma that offers countless opportunities throughout the day to respect mute objects and see them as teachers. Looked upon this way, should shoes and articles of clothing be just thrown about our living quarters? Should the items in our cupboards and desks exist in an indiscriminate state of disorder? What about items in our workplace? In our kitchen? They are our teachers, not only because they provide a focus for our awareness practice but because they are "radiantly expounding the Dharma without ceasing." Should we not listen to them? Should we not revere them?

Dongshan may have been listening but he could not hear. He still could not grasp how nonsentient things can teach, for teaching still meant words to him. So he did what we would probably do. He asked, "In which sutra is it taught that nonsentient beings expound the Dharma?" In other words, where is it written, where is it *proved*, who else said it apart from you, Master Yunyan? In response, Yunyan quoted the Amitabha Sutra, in which it says, "Water birds, tree groves, all without exception, recite the Buddha's name, recite the Dharma." Dongshan heard these words and in that mysterious way in which insight suddenly arises and one sees what previously could not be seen, he saw. His ego-mind cleared. Poet that he was, he expressed his insight in the following way:

How amazing, how amazing!
Hard to comprehend that nonsentient beings expound
the Dharma.

106

It simply cannot be heard with the ear,
But when the sound is heard with the eye, then it is
understood.

"How amazing, how amazing! Hard to comprehend." Are these not
the words—or similar ones—we also use when an insight opens up
for us? "It's unbelievable!" we say. "I can't understand it." Of course we
can't understand it, for it's not understandable—to the discriminating
ego-mind, that is. But just because it is not understandable to the ego-
mind does not mean that it is not understandable when that mind is
still. This understanding is deeper than ego-mind understanding, for it
sees through the limitations of the phenomenal world. It is an understanding that is heard with the eye and seen with the ear—which makes
complete sense when the discriminating mind is still. It is an understanding that easily "hears" and "sees" the Dharma taught by rocks and
trees—the Dharma of their essential nature. It is an understanding that
does not separate the essential nature of rocks and trees from rocks and
trees. Not-two. How amazing, how amazing!

Dongshan's pressing question had been resolved. He had awakened.
He no longer had to *hear* the Dharma (hear words) with his ear. But his
eye of enlightenment had opened only to a certain point. He grasped
the answer but did not yet fully realize it—a subtle distinction and an
essential one. The first layer of enlightenment, as we could call it, is to
grasp teaching with what we could call our "large mind." We understand in a way that is beyond our rational understanding, but there is
still a "me" understanding an "it." The full realization of this understanding happens when "me" and "it" drop away—something that was
not to happen to Dongshan until another time. The box did not yet fit
the lid. This does not mean, however, that the awakening expressed
in his "How amazing!" poem was not deep. It was. His gratitude to
Yunyan at that moment must have been heartfelt, and yet he chose not
to remain in the cave hermitage. Although he seems to have stayed for
a while with the master, whom he would always call his teacher (the lineage charts recognize Dongshan as Yunyan's Dharma heir), Dongshan
eventually felt he had to leave, just as he had previously left Nanquan

and Guishan. When Dongshan told the master about his decision, the following exchange took place:

> "Where are you going to go?" asked Yunyan.
> "I don't know where I'm going," replied Dongshan.
> "You're not going to Hunan [presumably back to Guishan's monastery]?"
> "No."
> "You're not going to your hometown?"
> "No."
> "Come back soon," said the master.
> "When you become head of a monastery I'll come back," said Dongshan.
> "Once you've gone, it will be difficult for us to see each other again."
> "It will be difficult for us not to see each other," replied Dongshan.

The last line of the dialogue above foreshadows Dongshan's upcoming full awakening. One senses a wonderful ease between these two, the ease of kindred spirits who both understand, who both see into the Great Matter. "Master" and "student" have both dropped away, and we see only two awakened people who respect each other greatly, who realize the necessity of parting, and who experience the sadness of such parting. They don't deny the depth of their feelings but don't get caught by these feelings either.

As Dongshan was leaving, he and Yunyan had a final exchange. Here is how it is described in *The Transmission of the Lamp*: "After you have passed away, how can I answer someone if he wants me to describe what you were like?" Dongshan asked. "You just say to him, 'This is!'" Yunyan replied. Dongshan was silent. He didn't yet fully understand. Yunyan then said to him, "You must be very careful, as you are carrying this great thing." And those were the words Dongshan was left with as he descended the mountain slope. One can only imagine his puzzlement on being told that he was "carrying this great thing." What could the great thing be, he must have wondered. Where and when will I find it? How do I need to be careful? But was it only Dongshan who carried "this great thing" or is it you and me? Do we too need to be careful? What could "this great thing" be? Pay attention!

SO DONGSHAN set out on pilgrimage once again, sometimes walking alone, sometimes with others. Pilgrimage was to be a major part of his life (over twenty years) and, as *The Record of Tung-shan* shows, he had far more exchanges with those he met on pilgrimage than he did with his teacher, Yunyan. Dongshan was indeed a seeker, constantly seeking to realize the truth through others, and although most of his teachers were formal Zen masters like those mentioned above, he also learned from unorthodox sources. When he first set out on pilgrimage, he met an old woman carrying water. He asked her for some water to drink. "You can have a drink," she replied, "but first, tell me, how dirty is the water?" "The water is not at all dirty," Dongshan said, probably checking out the water bucket first. "Go away. Don't pollute my water bucket," said the woman, and she walked on.

Dongshan was still caught in the world of phenomena, just as he had been caught in the limited phenomena of rocks and tiles. "Not stained, not pure," the Heart Sutra teaches. No discrimination. The Zen eye of "not-two" does not see either dirty or clean—only water. Don't pollute my water bucket with duality, the old woman (who may have been studying with some nearby Zen master) is saying. Don't place labels on anything—including me, she might have added, for women were considered impure in Buddhist doctrine and it was thought that they could not realize buddhahood. Don't buy into that, the woman is saying. I am not pure or impure. The water is not dirty or clean. Too bad you didn't answer correctly! How might an awakened Dongshan have answered the old woman? He could have taken out his bowl, scooped out some water, drunk it, and then bowed. But he was not yet awakened—and so he had to go on, thirsty.

The Record of Tung-shan recounts many such pilgrimage conversations between Dongshan and various teachers and fellow students, but one day something happened. Everything changed! He found himself crossing a stream. As he looked down, he saw his reflection, and his great awakening happened. As before, he expressed this in a poem:

> Avoid seeking elsewhere, for that's far from the self.
> Now I travel alone, everywhere I meet it.
> Now it's exactly me, now I'm not it.
> It must thus be understood to merge with thusness.

What a moment! After all that searching, all that traveling, after climbing those rocks and living in a cave, after all the questioning and exploration of the Great Matter with some of the finest Zen teachers living, after going thirsty on so many occasions, Dongshan had awakened—far from any monastic center, far from any teacher, far from any sutras, as he met his image in the water. His separating mind had dropped off, and he realized that "it" was exactly *he*, while at the same time he was not "it." For if he *was* "it" and "it" was he, then change and movement could not happen—reality would be static and still. Not-two, yet two. Same, yet different. Understanding this way—an understanding beyond mental understanding—is essential, Dongshan is telling us, in order to "to merge with thusness." "Thusness," in the Zen understanding of the word, is not a thing. It is a verb and it is alive. It is living. You must understand this way in order to merge with living as is—this is the teaching. Merge with living as is. When it's hot, be hot; when it's cold, be cold; when you sit, be sitting; when you breathe, be breathing; when you work, be working. Merge with living as is. This is "no-self living" or *tathagata*, another term for buddha. Dongshan had merged and he was liberated from ever again seeking outside of himself. He had awakened outside of words, outside of teachers, through the Dharma of nature.

"Now I travel alone." Dongshan's awakening also brought the deep realization that he was alone—that he was "all one." (Take away the letter "l" from *all one* and you have *alone*.) He realized there was nothing outside of himself and that he no longer had to seek from others, for there were no others outside of himself to seek from. *Alone* now had a whole new meaning for him. What meaning does it have for you? How do you feel about being alone? Is it a negative for you, as it is for so many people? Or is it liberation?

Whether or not Dongshan continued on his pilgrimage after this is not clear, but the wanderer did eventually settle down. *The Transmission of the Lamp* tells us that from 847 (when he would have been forty years old) until 859, he taught at Xinfeng Mountain, after which time he moved to Mount Dong—hence his name—Dongshan. Mount Dong was in Kiangsi Province, and so the man of pilgrimage settled down for the last ten years of his life, near those teachers who had in their own way supported and encouraged his awakening.

Dong means "cave" but it does not seem that Dongshan lived in caves, as did his teacher, Yunyan. Nor did he live in a hermitage like his predecessor, Shitou. *The Record of Tung-shan* describes a monastic center where people were seen off at the gate, various Zen masters are described as paying visits, exchanges with students happened in rice paddies and other outdoor places, monks tended a garden, the cook made soy paste in the kitchen, and there are references to monks going out to do manual labor. Manual labor was by then an established part of the monastic tradition, as we can see in the following anecdote. A government official visited the master and asked whether anyone was approaching Zen through cultivation (practice). Dongshan dryly replied, "When *you* become a laborer, then there will be someone to do cultivation." One wonders how the government official took that.

The Baizhang Zen Monastic Regulations made meditation the foundation of daily routine, in addition to the one-on-one teaching exchanges between master and student that now happened not only in the formal setting of the interview room but also in the daily life of the monastery. One day, for example, as Master Dongshan was washing his bowl (no attendants to wash the master's bowl here) he saw two birds fighting over a frog. A monk also witnessed this scene and asked, "Why does it come to that?" "Only for your benefit," Dongshan replied. This is the detached viewing of life's reality. There is no right or wrong when the discriminating mind is still. No meaning. Just this. It is for your benefit—to help you awaken.

Another time, after three of his students had finished sitting meditation, Dongshan brought them some tea (no attendant bringing tea here). One of them closed his eyes. "Where did you go?" asked Dongshan. "I entered *samadhi* [a deep state of concentration]." "Samadhi has no entrance. Where did you come from?" inquired the teacher. The student's response is not recorded. No separation. Here and there are one and the same.

One monk's question about how to deal with the weather brought a concise response. "How do you avoid the discomfort of hot and cold?" the monk asked. Master Dongshan said, "Go to that place where there is no hot and cold." "And where is that place?" queried the monk. The master said, "When you are hot, *be* hot, and when you are cold, *be* cold." In other words, the place of "not hot," "not cold," and "not pain" that we seek is the place of hot, cold, or pain we wish to avoid. The identical place. Choose to be one with the heat, the cold, the pain, Dongshan is saying, *be* it—no separation—and there will be no heat, no cold, no pain. It is the experience of "just this," with not a single layer of mind between oneself and the experience. Explore the experience without any descriptive words, thoughts, concepts, images, or feelings. One could call it the exploration of specific experiences with no mind whatsoever attached. In *zazen*, such wordless, imageless exploration of this moment's specific experience is called "just sitting" (*shikantaza* in Japanese). In life we could call it "just hot," "just cold," "just pain." It is the central experiential teaching of the Soto school but it took its founder, Dongshan Liangjie, many years of difficult practice to realize it.

DONGSHAN HAD TWENTY-SIX Dharma successors. The two foremost were Yunju Daoying (J. Ungo Doyo) and Caoshan Benji (J. Sozan Honjaku), and their part in the development of the Caodong (Soto) school is important. There are several recorded exchanges with Yunju in *The Record of Tung-shan* but Caoshan appears only once. Apparently he had been studying with the master (probably from 865–868) and, as he was about to leave, Dongshan gave him the text of a poem, "Jewel Mirror Samadhi," that Dongshan said had been entrusted to him by his own master, Yunyan. This poem, still chanted today in Soto Zen centers and monasteries, begins as follows:

> The Dharma of Suchness, directly transmitted by buddhas
>   and patriarchs,
> Today is yours; preserve it carefully.
> It is like a silver bowl heaped with snow and [like] the bright
>   moon concealing herons.
> When classified they differ, but lumped together their where-
>   abouts is known.

Later it says:

> Like gazing into the jewel mirror, form and reflection view each
>   other;
> You are not him, but he is clearly you.

These words are similar to Dongshan's own awakening poem, and both poems echo the words of Yunyan and Dongshan's ancestor, Shitou, in his poem "Identity of Relative and Absolute." Two and yet not-two.

Although it is not recorded, Dongshan must also have given Caoshan a teaching that Caoshan subsequently expanded into the famous dialectic formula of the Five Ranks. Simply put, the Five Ranks—not sequential steps but different viewpoints of enlightenment—are:

> Relative within absolute
> Absolute within relative
> Coming from within absolute
> Going within together
> Arriving within together

The Five Ranks formula was used by Caoshan in his teaching, and passed on in one way or another as part of the Caodong (Soto) school tradition. It came to be widely used in Zen circles and consequently, as Heinrich Dumoulin states, it "represents the most important dialectic formula in all of Zen Buddhism." The Five Ranks teaching continues to play an important part in Zen training to this day since, in the eighteenth century, the great Japanese Rinzai Zen master Hakuin Ekaku crossed traditions and used the Five Ranks of the Soto school as the focal point of the final fifty koans in his organized curriculum of koans.

Caoshan passed on Dongshan's teaching, first at a new temple in Fuzhou and later on Mount Heyu, and his reputation spread far and wide. Later his name came to be intimately linked with his teacher's name: the name of the Caodong school comes from *Caoshan* and *Dongshan* combined. It is the same in Japanese; *Soto* is formed from the merged first syllables of Sozan (Caoshan) and Tozan (Dongshan). What is significant, however, is that the actual Caodong line comes to us not through Caoshan (whose line ran out almost immediately), but through Dongshan's other prominent Dharma heir, Yunju, who did not teach the Five Ranks. After leaving Dongshan and spending time at Three Peak Hermitage, Yunju established Jenru (True Thusness Temple) on Mount Yunju where for thirty years he inspired large numbers of followers, passing on his master's primary teaching of two yet not-two.

Dongshan lived the direct experience of not-one, not-two to the very end. In the year 869 he became very ill. A monk came to pay his respects and asked the master if there was someone who was well. There was, said Dongshan. "Can the one who is well still see the master?" asked the monk. "I can still see him," said Dongshan. "What does the master see?" asked the monk. "When I observe him, I don't see any illness," Dongshan replied. When you are one with anything, can you see it? When you're hot, *be* hot; when you're cold, *be* cold; when you're ill, *be* ill.

Such clarity allowed for a most wonderful and even poignantly humorous rite of passing to take place as Dongshan approached his final days. Realizing that the end was near, he bathed, shaved, put on his robe, and began to pass away. Immediately all the monks started to wail and lament. Dongshan opened his eyes and said, "A mind unattached to things is the true practice. People struggle to live and make much of death. But what's the use of lamenting?" Yet the devoted monks, being human, kept on lamenting. Realizing that they needed a little more time to adjust, Dongshan ordered arrangements to be made for a "delusion banquet." A delusion banquet! Surely we have all participated in many such banquets ourselves. Preparations for the "delusion banquet" (whose main course might have been "Please don't die, master") were extended for seven days—and the master joined in the preparations. After seven days, however, realizing that they had to face reality, Dongshan sternly told his disciples, "You monks have made a great commotion over nothing. When you see me pass away *this* time, don't make a noisy fuss!" He then retired to his room, sat down, and died. He was sixty-two years old.

Where is Dongshan right now? Avoid looking elsewhere.

9. DESHAN

J. TOKUSAN; 782-865

IF YOU SPEAK, YOU GET THIRTY BLOWS;
IF YOU DON'T SPEAK, YOU GET THIRTY BLOWS

THE SCENE IS the dining area of a Zen monastery on Mount Te in Hunan Province, around the year 862. The cook, a forty-year-old monk named Xuefeng Yicun (J. Seppo Gison), is preparing the evening meal when he sees, shuffling down the corridor, the elderly abbot of the monastery carrying his bowls, as was customary, to dinner. "Master," he says, "the bell hasn't rung and the drum [to announce the meal] has not sounded. Why are you going to the dining room with your bowls?" On hearing this, the old man turns around and shuffles back to his room.

Extraordinary! Why? After all, the master was early, and he simply turned around. But if we were to meet this same Zen master some fifty years earlier, we would be hard pressed to recognize him. He probably would not have recognized himself.

But Zen does that—it changes you and turns you around so that you may look back and not recognize who that "you" was back then. Have you ever reflected in this way? It is a helpful undertaking every now and then, for it allows one to probe deeper the burning question "Who am I?" "Was that me?" you might ask. And, if not, is this me now? And will this me be the same a few years down the road? Just exactly who *is* this me anyway? Is there even a *me*? These questions help us probe deeper and deeper into the illusion of identity. Identity—the sense of a *me*—is created by the ego-mind, which from earliest childhood stitches together all the information that it receives from the outside about this

117

me and then continues, year after year, to grow a self, an ego, out of this very limited information. But is this *me*? The more we still this self-creating mind through practice, the more we begin to question this *me* and so begin to realize who we really are—larger, deeper, vaster, and, in fact, not a separate *me* after all. Yes, Zen turns you around. It certainly turned this old bowl-carrying Zen master around dramatically.

HIS NAME WAS DESHAN XUANJIAN (J. Tokusan Senkan), born in northern China in 782, eight years before the death of Shitou, whose great-grandson in the Dharma he was to become. As a young monk, after his initial study of the Vinaya (the Buddhist disciplines), as well as the sutras (Buddhist scriptures), he became what could be called "a professional lecturer," for he made his living giving talks, especially on the text that was his specialty, the Diamond Sutra. It is a major wisdom sutra of Mahayana Buddhism, developed between the years 300 and 500, and it points to direct experience of "suchness," beyond words and meaning; it is the diamond that cuts through the delusions of limited ego-mind. It is the same text that Huineng, the sixth ancestor, heard in the marketplace when he was a poor woodcutter at the beginning of his Zen odyssey. But Huineng and Deshan had vastly different responses to the sutra. Huineng realized the truth it was pointing to, while Deshan only understood it intellectually and lectured about it. In fact, he became so renowned for his erudition on this sutra that he became known as Diamond Chou—Chou being his surname. One suspects that he took pleasure in this title and was proud of his teaching, for Deshan was a highly energetic, zealous, and sometimes brash young man in his late twenties or early thirties who in many ways thought he had all the answers.

The irony was that he was talking about a teaching that clearly states that there is nothing to talk about. Everything just is, and *is-ness* can have nothing outside of itself to be viewed as an object. Deshan, however, had made *nothing*, or *emptiness*, into a thing to be grasped by the ego-mind—the very mind that the text said was empty. But he could not see this because his knowledge-filled ego-mind obstructed his clear vision—as it does ours. We, like Deshan, can come to understand the Dharma, and indeed we *must* first understand it, because conceptual understanding is the gateway to awakening. But understanding is not direct experience, and to remain only at the level of understanding is not Zen insight, just as talking about swimming is not swimming. In order to grasp what swimming is, we must experience it, and in order to grasp what emptiness is we must experience emptiness directly by stilling the discriminating ego-mind.

Deshan, however, oblivious to the contradiction that he was only talking about a teaching on direct experience, moved confidently around northern China giving his lectures. He was devoted to study and devoted to the Diamond Sutra, and so when he heard of a fairly new school of Buddhism in the south called Chan, which taught that awakening was possible only outside of the sutras and the teachings, he became indignant, not only because he believed that awakening came through study and teachings but because the Diamond Sutra was one of this new sect's favorite texts. It was the sutra through which its founder, Huineng, had first come to awakening. "They're co-opting my sutra," he must have thought, "and using it to teach that there is no need of study and teaching and lectures. This is wrong." So Deshan, more zealous than ever, resolved to stamp out what he perceived to be not only a heresy but also a direct threat to his livelihood as a lecturer. He packed up his precious notes and commentaries and began his journey south, crossing the Yangtze River and probably giving a few talks along the way. He was indignant, passionate, single-minded, and self-righteous. In this he is similar to the apostle Paul before his dramatic conversion to the way of Jesus of Nazareth. Like Deshan, Paul thought that the new "Jesus sect" springing up around the Mediterranean was corrupting Judaism, and he felt it was his mission to stamp it out. Like Deshan, he was self-righteous, convinced that he had the answers while everyone else was wrong.

In general we tend to view self-righteousness as bad and unhealthy, but perhaps it's not all bad—provided we don't linger there for too long. "I am right" is a necessary part of a developing sense of self, a developing sense of a healthy ego, of one's specificity and one's unique knowing. We are not meant to be neutral—we are meant to be specific. Shitou's "Identity of Relative and Absolute," examined in an earlier chapter, clearly teaches this, and we must develop great confidence in our specificity and our view of the world before we can let it go. The Buddha would not have wanted otherwise, for he charged his disciples (us) to trust in themselves and not be slaves of other people's points of view. Too many people come to Zen trying to let go of a self they haven't found yet. In our awakening journey we must be allowed to be "self-right," provided we are open to its challenger—doubt.

Doubt is what Deshan met soon after crossing into southern China, and the doubt was instigated by an unlikely thing—a dumpling. On coming to Lizhou in Hunan Province, he stopped by a small roadside stand selling dumplings. It was run by an old woman who, unknown to Deshan, may have been something of a Zen adept, living as she did near the monastery of a well-known Zen master, maybe even being a lay student of his. There Deshan asked for *tenjin*, or "something to eat." In Chinese the characters for *ten* and *jin* mean "pointing to mind." So *tenjin* is both "something to eat" and "pointing to mind." How wonderful! Dumplings are pointing to mind! Deshan asked for dumplings and the woman began a conversation:

> "Reverend monk, what are you carrying there in your heavy pack?"
>
> "Oh, those are my notes and lectures on the Diamond Sutra. I am an expert on this sutra. I'm well known for my interpretation of its meaning."
>
> "Oh, really? Well, I will ask you a question and, if you can answer this question, you will get the *tenjin* for free."
>
> "Wonderful!" replied Deshan, perhaps with a small smile of satisfaction at the prospect of a free meal. "Ask away."
>
> "Well, reverend monk, in the Diamond Sutra it says that past mind cannot be grasped [is unknowable], present mind cannot be grasped, and future mind cannot be grasped. Which mind are you pointing to? Which mind is eating the *tenjin*?"

What a fabulous question, posed by an unlikely Zen master not caught by sutras and teachings. Which mind are you pointing to?

The Diamond Sutra cuts through the illusion of "mind." There is no separately existing mind, there is no separately existing *anything*, but Deshan only knew about this, he had not *realized* it, and so he was still caught in the illusion of "mind" as a separate thing. And he was totally taken aback. He could not answer and for the first time he met doubt. The bubble of self-righteousness was penetrated. We can be so self-righteous about so many things—Zen, our practice, our knowledge, our point of view—and we too must allow our self-righteous bubble to be broken by stopping short, as did Deshan, and saying, in so many words, "I don't know the answer."

Which mind are you pointing to? Which mind eats? The mind is not a separate thing. As the Heart Sutra puts it, emptiness is form and form is emptiness. Forms exist. Dumplings exist. Emptiness is not emptiness, it is form. Deshan, like so many of us, saw emptiness as a thing, mind as a thing—objects to be pondered and lectured on. But emptiness and mind are "no-things," only *this* thing, this dumpling thing. Such truth can be seen only if the ego-mind, creator of "things" as objects, is stilled. Deshan was trying to grasp the ungraspable with his limited ego-mind and could not answer. He probably felt very foolish and embarrassed, as do we when we can't answer a Zen question, though we must always remember that feeling foolish and embarrassed, however unpleasant, is really a very good thing, for it sharply pierces our self-righteous ignorance.

It certainly could not have been pleasant for Deshan to be embarrassed (by an old woman, no less), but he soon regained his confidence and, being the bright person he was, probably thought something like this: "Perhaps this woman has been influenced by this Chan I've come to investigate (the one that's taken over my specialty sutra) and so I need to find one of these Chan masters against whom I can test my theories. Perhaps I'll do better with him than with this woman." (Oh, really?) And so he asked her if there was a Zen master in the vicinity. "Oh, yes," she told me, "as a matter of fact there is a great teacher named Master Longtan Chongxin (J. Ryutan Soshin) just a few miles up the road. Why don't you go visit him?" "I will," said Deshan, "for I have heard of this teacher and want to meet him." So he left. History does not record if the old woman was kind and gave him the dumpling for free anyway. Probably not—tea-shop ladies were pretty fierce. And how would have an awakened Deshan answered the old woman's statement? Perhaps he would have picked up the dumpling, taken a bite, and said, "Madam, this dumpling is delicious. Thank you for the free lunch!" But he was not awakened—not yet.

As he walked down the road toward Longtan's monastery, Deshan's brash confidence must have returned for when he arrived at the gate it was on display in full force. Longtan's name is made up of two Chinese characters, meaning "dragon" and "deep water," and so, upon arrival, Deshan called out in a loud voice, "I have long heard the name Longtan but I see no dragon and I see no deep water." He probably felt pretty full of himself at this pithy expression of "emptiness," for he knew that everything is empty—he just had not realized that emptiness does not exist outside of form. Form soon appeared in the shape of Dragon Deep Water himself (Longtan), who had come to see who was making all the commotion. He opened the gate and said to the young monk in front of him, "You have your Dragon Deep Water now." *This* is emptiness, he was saying. Deshan did not perceive this subtle teaching but, as with the encounter with the old woman, something may have stirred. "Is this Zen teacher trying to tell me something?" he might have thought. "If so, I don't see what it is." Doubt again? Perhaps—but he was willing to keep going.

Deshan was invited in, as were all traveling seekers of the time, but he was not content to take things slowly. That evening he went to the master's room and they entered into what appears to have been a marathon conversation. (The events of that evening are revisited in koan 28 of *The Gateless Gate*.) It's probable that Deshan kept trying to prove the necessity of study as the path to awakening, with Longtan listening graciously. But Deshan was met at every turn by the master's incisive responses, delivered through the teaching method of answering a question with another question, probably inspired by his Dharma grandfather, Shitou. This eventually began to wear on Deshan, and he may have begun to grasp that maybe there was something to this Chan way, when poor Longtan, weary of having this bundle of energy in the room for so long, said that it was time for both of them to retire. As Deshan moved into the darkness, the master gave him a lantern to guide him on his path but when Deshan took it the master blew out the light. Deshan was struck as if by lightning! His ego-mind that had for so long guided him in his quest for knowledge dropped off; it was metaphorically blown out. He saw clearly that there was no knowledge to gain, nothing to know, and that knowing *this* was "knowing" everything. He bowed deeply to the master.

What brilliant teaching on Longtan's part. There were no words, no lectures, no stacks of commentaries, no sutras needed. Just using the moment at hand with a highly gifted student who was primed and ready. The blazing truth is that there is no light, there is no way, there is nothing to search for, nothing to find. There is no meaning, because *everything* is meaning. Just sit, just walk, just eat, just sleep, just work. Each moment is complete. Simple! And Deshan got it, for he was like a ripe fruit ready to drop. Fruit ripens by itself and though he did not know it he was ripening all the time he was studying the Diamond Sutra, all the time he was lecturing on it, all the time he was traveling down the Yangtze, and surely when he was held up by a dumpling. His mind had dropped off, and all the sutras and teachings dropped off with it. He had met the "heresy" and found the heresy to be true. Awakening *is* outside of sutras and teachings. He bowed deeply. "What have you seen that you bow?" asked the master. "Never to doubt the teachings of the venerable teachers of the world," replied Deshan. Why will he never doubt the venerable teachers? Because he had finally realized their teachings for himself. He would not follow Longtan blindly as he followed the Diamond Sutra blindly. He realized the seismic difference between the two, as do we when we move from knowing something to *realizing* it.

At last Master Longtan and Deshan went to get some sleep, though it's doubtful if Deshan slept much that night. The next day, the master, probably still a little tired, said to the morning assembly of monks, which now included Deshan, "Among you is a fellow with fangs like swords. If you beat him, he won't flinch. He is firm and reliable and will, one day, establish the Way." Then Deshan's volatile personality came on display again. Instead of quietly staying with his newly found insight, he displayed it dramatically. He took his big bag of commentaries and his precious sutras and in front of the whole assembly declared, "Even if you attain all the knowledge in the world, it's like a drop of water in a deep ravine." Then he took a torch and set fire to all his "knowledge." Quite a showman, was he not, even in enlightenment? We can only presume that the hall did not burn down. The record is not clear as to what happened next except that "later" (that day? in a month? in a year?) he was off to meet another well-known Zen master.

This was Guishan Lingyou, whom we met earlier, and who, at the time of Deshan's visit, seems to have been relatively young and in the early years of his new position as abbot of the monastery on Mount Gui. Here's what happened, as recounted in koan 4 of *The Blue Cliff Record*.

It was early morning and the monks were preparing for meditation in the hall when Deshan walked in. He was wearing his dusty traveling clothes, which was not a respectful thing to do when calling on a Zen master, but this was Deshan, impulsive as ever. He strode into the center of the hall and cried out, "Is it here? Is it here?" Master Guishan paid him no heed. "No, no," cried Deshan, and he walked out. Another great drama. What is this about? Is "it" here? Of course not. If "it" were in the meditation hall, the church, or the synagogue, if it were in nature, then there would be somewhere where "it" was not. "It" is everywhere and everything, so "it" is nowhere and nothing. In this grand gesture in the meditation hall, Deshan was expressing his deep realization of the emptiness of the universe outside of sutras and teachings, but his expression was not yet complete. This time, however, he realized it himself, no longer needing a candle or a *tenjin*. As he reached the front gate, he suddenly stopped and said to himself, "Wait a minute. That was a bit crude," and he returned. What was crude? Disrespect for the master and assembly, yes, but more importantly his expressed insight was crude. "It" is not here, and yet it is. Emptiness is form and form is emptiness. To believe that the "emptiness of all that is" is license to behave any way one wants is erroneous. Emptiness is structure and form; emptiness is ritual and paying respects. Deshan had now realized this.

So he changed his traveling clothes for more formal attire and returned to the meditation hall where Guishan was about to give his Dharma talk. Deshan walked up to him, bowed deeply, and said, "Master." Emptiness is not emptiness. At that very moment, it was "the master." Deshan had expressed his realization fully. At this, Guishan raised his fly whisk, the same one he had raised for Dongshan, upon which Deshan gave a shout, pulled back his sleeve, and walked out. As we have seen in earlier chapters, the shout is a spontaneous expression of the Zen spirit, cutting off all concepts. So here Deshan vividly demonstrated how all concepts, all authority, must be cut off. There is no authority, no Master Guishan, *and* I bow to him. Guishan, as a Dharma grandson of Mazu, would have been very familiar with this shout and surely knew he had just encountered the real thing in this unorthodox stranger. Later that evening he asked his head monk whether "that fellow who came today" was still here. On being told he had left, the master said, "That fellow will go to the top of a high peak, build a grass hut, and revile the buddhas and ancestors." Which is exactly what Deshan proceeded to do.

What does Deshan teach us here? Through his actions, he demonstrates that we too must cut off all the authorities in our life that run us—the outer authorities, as well as the inner authorities of our "shoulds" and "oughts." Kill the Buddha, kill the teacher, Guishan's Dharma nephew, Linji, was teaching at this very time. We must learn to do this. Have confidence in yourself, Deshan teaches, confidence in your own way of seeing and expressing reality. Be who you are and never try to be someone you are not. Don't try to become an enlightened person, just *be*. Zazen is already enlightenment. Trust the experience of your still mind. Live single-mindedly. Be alive. Above all, be courageously committed, for you are on your own on this journey. The French writer Marcel Proust intuited this when he wrote, "We do not receive wisdom. We must discover it for ourselves after a journey through the wilderness which no one else can make for us, which no one else can spare us. For our wisdom is the point of view from which we come, at last, to regard the world."

Trust yourself. Do it your way. Deshan certainly did things his own way, and his next step was no exception: he dropped out of sight for about thirty years, "dwelling in obscurity" in Hunan, as *The Transmission of the Lamp* tells us. The only other information we have in this record is that in the year 845, during the Buddhist persecutions carried out by Emperor Wuzong, Deshan "escaped to a stone grotto on a mountain." It is hard to imagine the extroverted and impulsive Deshan not only going into obscurity but remaining there for such a long time, and yet this makes sense. For his awakening experience with the blown-out candle was total—he "died"—and for a single-minded person such as he, a "death" like this must be truly lived out. How inspiring! Would that we could aspire to just a fraction of such dedicated trust in the Way. Deshan escaped to the mountains and would have probably ended his life there had he not been called by circumstances, which greatly echo the journey of his ancestor Shitou.

SHORTLY AFTER THE END of the 845 persecutions, when the subsequent emperor reversed earlier measures and allowed Buddhist services to resume and a limited number of temples to be rebuilt, the governor of Hunan Province restored the monastery on Mount De. Looking around for some worthy teacher to be the abbot, he heard of Deshan and invited him to be the Chan master of this temple. Iconoclastic as ever, Deshan refused to leave his mountain hermitage despite repeated invitations. Finally the governor made up a story about Deshan's having broken some laws regarding the consumption of tea and salt and summoned him to explain himself. The trick apparently worked, for Deshan traveled to the governor's place. Once there, the governor treated him with great reverence, begging him to stay and to reveal the teachings of Chan. He must have been quite persuasive, for the next we hear of Deshan is in his role as master of Mount De Temple, after which he took his name. There he remained for the next fifteen years or so, until his death in 865.

It would be a mistake to believe that Deshan's thirty years in obscurity had mellowed him. On the contrary, the master on Mount De was as rigorous and fierce as ever. He became famous for his teaching of the thirty blows: "If you speak, you get thirty blows. If you don't speak, you get thirty blows." Put another way, "As soon as you ask, you have erred. If you don't ask, you're wrong also." Where does that leave you? Nowhere. Exactly. Just where the master wants you to be. Part of one of Deshan's talks underscores this strict teaching: "If you have no affairs in your mind, nor mind in your affairs, then you are unoccupied yet animated, empty, and wondrous. But if you allow yourself to stray from this upright state, all words [or lack of words, one could add] will deceive you." It is not about thirty blows or no thirty blows, both of which involve the discriminating mind of either/or. It is not "either/or," it is always "just this." And "just this" is your life. Here are three passages attributed to Deshan:

> What is known as "realizing the mystery" is nothing but breaking through to grab an ordinary person's life.
>
> Here, there are no ancestors and no buddhas. Bodhidharma is an old stinking foreigner, Shakyamuni is a dried piece of excrement.
>
> A monk asked, "Is there much difference between sacred and ordinary?" Deshan gave a shout.

Yes, Deshan was fierce, but he drew many followers and had a number of Dharma successors, reenergizing a secondary line of succession from Shitou, which was to include Xuefeng, Yunmen, and Fayan, all of whom we will meet in the coming chapters. Deshan's students instinctively understood that his uncompromising stance was the true way, for he was now fully expressing the wisdom teaching of the Diamond Sutra which he had once only understood as a concept. There is no wisdom to attain because everything is wisdom; there is no buddha to aspire to because everything is buddha. "It" is just an ordinary person's life.

All this brings us to the scene that opened this chapter. Knowing the younger Deshan, we would be hard pressed to recognize the old, shuffling master coming early to dinner and then quietly turning around when told of his mistake. And we would be right, for it is not the same person. Everything changes, everything evolves. Deshan's ego-self had truly dropped off by now and he was totally in the moment. The twentieth-century Zen master Zenkei Shibayama Roshi, in his commentary on koan 13 in *The Gateless Gate*, in which this story appears, describes Deshan's moment outside the dining hall in the following way: "There is no stink of Zen [here]. He lives with no pretension, no affectation. His transcendental purity is like that of an infant. Nobody can easily reach such spirituality." Deshan did reach such spirituality because he had practiced very hard. He had shown up every step of the way and had never flinched. The master, who had plenty of pretension and affectation in his youth, had now completely disappeared—into no-self living.

In such wholeness, there would have been no need to burn the sutras, no need to dismiss Guishan's authority, no need to sit on a solitary peak. But Deshan had to go through all that in order to realize this—and it seems to me that this is the in-depth teaching of that brief monastic moment in the dining area. Although everything is already complete, we have to go through different stages of discovering the truth of two and not-two for ourselves. We have to practice what we intuit, have to show up, have to be committed and even uncompromising. We have to be single-minded and, what Deshan models so fully, we have to be passionate. We must also be aware of our own different stages of development. We must know where we are and not be impatient about being somewhere we are not. We must accept things as they are and not lose heart when things get difficult. We must move slowly and carefully but we must also take risks. We must never cease striving. Above all, we must listen to our own inner drummer each step of the way. When we do all of this, we, like Deshan, will be carried by life, whichever way it takes us—like a leaf being carried down a stream. Living this way, like Deshan, we will be serene, transparent, leaving no traces. This last stage, exemplified in the monastery dining area, is not about being a doormat. It is the full realization that everything is empty, as the Diamond Sutra teaches, and therefore that everything is sacred, special, and of the utmost importance.

A short while later, in 865, Deshan died. Diamond Chou had finally realized his beloved Diamond Sutra.

10. Xuefeng

J. SEPPO; 822-908

IN THE LACQUER BUCKET, WHERE IS IT HARD TO SEE?

FAILURE: unless it's deliberately orchestrated for nefarious reasons, as in the Mel Brooks classic comedy *The Producers*, we would all probably agree that failure is something we would like to avoid. To be a failure in anything we undertake is synonymous with being not good enough or lacking something we feel we ought to know or possess. When failure happens to us we don't like it and we judge ourselves—often harshly and endlessly. "I'm so stupid! Why did I do that? Why can't I do what they can do? What will people think of me?" And so on. We all have our particular litanies. Sadly, such judgment doesn't stop with the judgment itself, for most of the time calling oneself a failure leads to loss of confidence, self-censoring, anger, shame, self-hatred, and other negative effects. Going in the opposite unhealthy direction, it can drive one to work harder, do more, succeed at all costs in order to avoid failure the next time—no matter what it takes. People like success, they don't like failure. The engine of the industrialized world runs on success; to fail is to be a nobody.

Zen practitioners are not exempt from failure but, strange as it may seem, failure is actually a necessary component of waking up. Everyone who comes to Zen has ideas of what Zen should be or what it should "produce." Yet all of these ideas have to fail, for that's all they are—ideas. They are creations of the conditioned mind's discriminating judgments, judgments that are continually placed on our actions or the actions of others. But actions are just actions—they are neither a success nor a failure. And this means that in Zen the illusory ideals of success created by the ego-mind have to constantly fail if we are to awaken. Failure is offered by the teacher as encouragement that one is on the right path. Whenever a student is ready to begin koan study with me, I always ask him or her, "Are you ready to meet failure? Because you will and you must." Failing is a hallmark of Zen practice.

Zen failures, are you ready to meet your hero? Are you ready to meet Zen Master Xuefeng Yicun (J. Seppo Gison), who, in his quest for awakening, underwent setbacks and failures that would have turned most of us off Zen entirely? How would you, after scrambling up to the mountain hut of a famous teacher and expressing what you were sure was the enlightened response to his question, like to be called "a black lacquer bucket" (a metaphor for pitch-black ignorance)? And four different times, no less. And this with just one teacher—there were others. But Xuefeng endured, prevailed, and eventually became the most respected Zen master in southern China in his time. It was said in Zen circles in the latter part of the ninth century, "Zhaozhou in the North, Xuefeng in the South." Zen failures, take heart.

Xuefeng Yicun was born in 822 in Fujian Province in the southeastern part of China. The record tells us that he seemed to have a predilection for the Buddha Way from an early age. When he was only twelve he went with his father to visit a Vinaya master and upon meeting him immediately bowed to him as "my master." He stayed in this monastery until the age of seventeen, serving as an attendant, but he did not receive ordination until eleven years later when, at the relatively old age of twenty-eight, he took his monastic vows at Baocha Monastery in Youzhou (the area around modern Beijing). Despite his early attraction to the Way, Xuefeng was what one might call a late bloomer. After ordination he was determined to realize enlightenment and began traveling on a pilgrimage, from Zen master to Zen master. The Blue Cliff Record tells us that at each monastery he visited he would set up his bucket, take out his wooden spoon, and serve as rice cook (a lowly position), simply to be able to have the opportunity to explore the Great Matter. One gets the picture of an extremely earnest young man, willing to do anything, even the most menial jobs, visiting many teachers and deter-mined to "succeed" at Zen.

He not only visited many teachers, he revisited them. Three times he went to see Master Touzi Datong (J. Tosu Daido), who lived in obscurity in a thatched hut on Mount Touzi, and three times he left, his arduous journey up the mountain proving fruitless each time. Touzi is the one who four times pronounced Xuefeng to be that "black lacquer bucket." In one of those exchanges Touzi pointed to a rock outside his hut and said, "All past, present, and future Buddhas are here." "Ah, but there is one who is not here," replied Xuefeng, demonstrating what he thought was his insight into the emptiness of all that is. Unfortunately, all he demonstrated was duality; in Oneness, no one can not be here. "You black lacquer bucket!" shouted the master. Another wrong answer! Zen practitioners involved in koan work can surely empathize. Failure can really hurt, but that's the way of the Way.

Among several others, Xuefeng also went to see Master Dongshan, whom we met earlier. Nine times he came, nine times he left, after being unable to answer the master's penetrating questions. Xuefeng worked hard at his kitchen duties and was always punctual in serving the morning meal but could not seem to break through in resolving the Great Matter. One day, for example, carrying in some firewood, he threw it on the ground. Dongshan was nearby and saw his teaching opportunity. "How heavy is the firewood?" he asked. "There is nobody in the whole world who could lift it [for it is empty, being the implica-tion]." "Then how did it get here?" asked the master. It must have been tough to be a student at Dongshan's place. You were stumped not only in the interview room but he caught you in the kitchen, too.

During the ninth visit, on a day when Xuefeng was straining the rice, Dongshan came along. Seeing an opening for a question, the master asked the cook, "Do you strain the rice from the sand or the sand from the rice?" "Rice and sand are both strained out at the same time," replied Xuefeng, again showing what he thought was insight into the empti-ness of all that is. "So then," asked the master, "what will the monks eat?" Good question. Xuefeng tipped over the pot. "Go," sighed Dong-shan. "Go to Deshan's place. He's the teacher for you." (You will recall that Deshan, whom we met in the last chapter, lived a long time in the illusion of emptiness.) So Xuefeng, bucket and wooden ladle in hand, set out for Deshan's place. Did he know, one wonders, what was in store for him at the monastery of the Master of the Thirty Blows? Whether he did or not, it is pretty clear that it would not have stopped him.

As he was setting out, he had the following exchange with Dongshan:

> "Where are you going?" asked the master.
> "I'm returning to Lingzhong."
> "When you left Lingzhong to come here, what road did you take?"
> "I took the road through the Flying Ape Mountains."
> "And what road are you taking to go back there?"
> "I'm returning through the Flying Ape Mountains as well."
> "There's someone who doesn't take the road through Flying Ape Mountains. Do you know him?"
> "I don't know him."
> "Why don't you know him?"
> "Because he doesn't have a face."
> "If you don't know him, how do you know he doesn't have a face?"
> Xuefeng was silent.

Poor fellow. To miss it, even after nine visits.

Who is it who didn't take the road through the Flying Ape Mountains? One is reminded of a poem by the great Japanese Zen poet, Basho:

> No one walks this path
> this autumn night.

No one takes the path, no one takes the road. No self living, no self walking. Who is the nobody reading this page?

UPON HIS ARRIVAL at Deshan's monastery, Xuefeng found two old friends with whom he had gone on pilgrimage for a time in the past—Yantou Quanhuo (J. Ganto Zenkatsu) and Qinshan Wensui (J. Kinzan Bunsui), both of whom were now studying with Deshan. Ultimately, Qinshan did not remain with Deshan, whose teaching methods were too harsh for him. He went to study with Dongshan, with whom he awakened and whose Dharma heir he eventually became—another example of the dynamic flow of Zen practitioners among the different Zen masters. Yantou, however, stayed and awakened under Deshan. He was six years younger than Xuefeng but became kind of a Dharma elder brother to the older man, trying to devise ways of helping Xuefeng to awaken. The story recounted in koan 13 in *The Gateless Gate* was one such attempt.

It begins with the scene, described in the previous chapter, of Deshan coming down to the dining room for the midday meal. He was an old man by now, not the energetic firebrand who had engaged the tea-shop lady about dumplings. Xuefeng, who had naturally taken on kitchen duties, saw the master and told him he was early, since the meal bell had not rung. Deshan just turned around and went back to his room. Yantou, being nearby, saw this as an opportunity to help his friend to awaken. "Poor old master," he remarked to Xuefeng, "he doesn't understand the last word of Zen." That must have caught Xuefeng's attention. "Have I outsmarted the master?" he might have thought, followed by, "But how did I do it? What *is* the last word of Zen?" Deshan, meanwhile, heard of Yantou's remark and called him to his room. "Don't you approve of me?" he asked. Yantou explained his intent to help Xuefeng. Would the master play along? Of course. Next day Deshan gave a Dharma talk quite different from any other. Yantou clapped his hands in front of the assembly and purely for Xuefeng's sake cried out, "How wonderful! The master has realized the last word of Zen. Now he'll be subject to nobody." But Xuefeng did not get it. "How did the master realize the last word? What *is* the last word?" he might have thought. Do you get it? What *is* the last word of Zen? There is a good reason that Master Mumon, who compiled *The Gateless Gate*, chose this story as part of his koan collection.

Years later, after he had awakened, Xuefeng lived alone for a time in a small hut. Two monks came to pay their respects. Xuefeng saw them coming, opened the door, came out, and said, "What is it?" One of the monks repeated, "What is it?" Xuefeng went back inside. Later this monk went to visit Yantou and told him the story. Yantou said, "Too bad I didn't tell him the last word before. If I had told him, he would be subject to nobody." The monk did not understand and he left, but it obviously gnawed at him because he came back for instruction about this matter. "If you want to know the last word," said Yantou, "just this is it." What a kind old grandmother Yantou was by now. He wasn't so helpful to Xuefeng, was he? No, he wasn't, and that's why Xuefeng struggled on at Deshan's monastery, toiling in the kitchen, receiving Deshan's blows in the interview room but still not seeing into the true nature of reality. Poor old Xuefeng. It seemed to be so easy for Yantou, why was it so hard for him? One wonders how he felt about his friend's seemingly effortless path. It must have been difficult to see Yantou shine while he kept plodding along.

Do we not know that feeling? How often do we perceive others in the sangha to be better practitioners than we are? How often do we perceive coworkers to be better at their jobs than we are? Do we not wonder how they seem to understand so clearly, to perform so well when we can't? Do we not compare? Surely Xuefeng must have compared, not only here at Deshan's but at the many other monastic centers where he continually seemed to meet failure while others seemed to meet success. What could he teach us in this regard? What kind of model might he be? It seems almost obvious that the reason so many more stories of his shortcomings were recorded and passed down—more than for any of the other ancestors, all of whom surely had many tough encounters in the interview room and elsewhere—was to inspire practitioners who followed, whether Chinese monks of the time or you and me. These stories were passed down to help us keep going, to not be discouraged, to withstand failure and seeming stupidity, to be content with being the tortoise and not the hare. Zen plodders, be encouraged. Don't give up. If Xuefeng could eventually awaken, so can you.

Here is how his awakening began. One day he came to the interview room and asked Deshan, in what must surely have been a plaintive voice, "Can *I* also attain what the ancestors attained?" Deshan hit him with his stick. "What are you talking about?" he cried out. Xuefeng later said that when this happened it was "like the bottom falling out of a bucket." That moment, when the bottom falls out of the bucket, is surely familiar to Zen practitioners—the awakening moment when something opens up (though often we don't fully know what). Something had opened up for Xuefeng but he still did not realize it fully. He left the interview room but came back the next day and asked again, "Can I also attain 'it'?" This time Deshan was a little kinder. He spoke words rather giving blows. "Zen has no words, neither does it have anything to give." Something probably shifted for Xuefeng but he still could not fully understand. He recounted the interview to Yantou who simply said, "Deshan has an iron backbone but he spoils Zen with his soft words."

Eventually Xuefeng did fully awaken, but not under Deshan, who passed away in 865. Although Xuefeng is considered to be Deshan's Dharma heir, his full awakening actually happened later under his friend Yantou. How fitting for them both.

The two were on another pilgrimage when they became snowbound at an inn on Tortoise Mountain in Li Province. Yantou spent the whole day sleeping while Xuefeng sat diligently in meditation. After a couple of days, this really began to bother Xuefeng. He went to his sleeping friend and shook him, crying, "Get up, get up! Don't be so lazy! We monks on pilgrimage have a grave responsibility! Great wisdom is our companion but all *you* do is sleep!" Yantou, obviously not appreciating having been woken, yelled back, "Stop carrying on! Just eat and sleep [just live your life]. Sitting in meditation all day is like being a statue in a villager's hut. If you go on like this, you'll just confuse people." Xuefeng responded, "I have a heaviness in my chest. I *can't* stop meditating all the time." Yantou tried to reassure him. "You'll be a great teacher one day. Don't go on like this." "I'm really anxious," Xuefeng responded. Sensing that perhaps something might be opening up, Yantou said, "Look, tell me your understanding of the Great Matter. Where it's correct, I'll affirm it, where it's incorrect, I'll point that out." Xuefeng agreed to do this.

"I found an entry with one teacher when I heard him talk about emptiness and form."

"Not it! [This is still an idea!]"

"Well, then I had another opening when I read Dongshan's poem: 'Avoid seeking elsewhere, for that's far from the Self, now I travel alone, everywhere I meet it, now it's exactly me, now I'm not it.'"

"Not yet! [This is someone else's insight!]"

"Well, then I had an interview with Deshan and I asked him, 'Can I also share in the ultimate teaching the old ancestors attained?' He hit me and it was like the bottom falling out of a bucket."

[Yantou must have sensed that Xuefeng was like a ripe apple about to drop off the tree.]

"Haven't you heard it said that 'what comes in through the front gate isn't the family treasure'?" he said to his friend.

"What should I do then?"

"In the future, if you want to express the great teaching, then it must flow out of *you* [the teaching must be yours—trust yourself]!"

And Xuefeng awakened. The bottom once again fell out of the bucket—this time totally—and the bucket was a black lacquer bucket of failure no more. He bowed deeply to his friend. "Elder brother," he said to the younger man, "at last today on Tortoise Mountain I've realized the Way."

He had realized there is no Way to attain, for it is already here. And perhaps he wept—as we often do when the fog clears, when the bottom falls out of our "black lacquer bucket of not seeing" and we see. More importantly, we trust what we see. Perhaps Yantou wept, as well. The kindness, generosity, and encouragement of this true bodhisattva had finally allowed his friend to awaken. What a moment for them both on that snowy mountain.

Trust yourself. This admonition is central to awakening because what we awaken to is our very self—our essential self. We do not awaken to someone else's essential self—how could we? We can only awaken to our own essential self. But if we don't trust it, if we don't act upon what this essential self reveals in the specific details of our lives, our insight goes nowhere. This lack of trust and consequent inaction, which happens when insight is swamped by doubt, is very common among Zen practitioners, resulting in indecision and being stuck. "This teaching [this insight] must flow out of *you*." Yantou's turning words spoken to Xuefeng are addressed to us, as well. Someone else's insight is not your insight. You must keep practicing with ever greater resolve, seeking to still the ego-mind, which creates doubts, until the bottom falls out of your bucket and, as Zen master Shitou said, "The box fits the lid." "How will I know when the box fits the lid?" Zen students often ask. You will know, believe me. How do you know that a glass of water on a hot day tastes good? How do you know that you connect when you meet a person on your wavelength? How do you know there is no separation between you and a Renoir painting, a Mozart symphony, or a Bruce Springsteen song? You know; you just know.

Yantou became an inspiring Zen teacher in his own right, drawing many monks to study with him at Yantou Monastery in Ezhou. Sadly, though, his life came to a tragic end. In 887, as chaos from the closing years of the Tang dynasty permeated the countryside, bandits were everywhere and some eventually came close to Yantou's monastic compound. All the monks fled except the master. He alone remained—meditating. When the head of the bandit gang came to the temple and found nothing of worth he became enraged and stabbed Yantou with his knife. Yantou was composed but let out a resounding scream as he died—a scream, it was said, heard for miles around. Surely Xuefeng, who outlived him by eleven years, must have grieved mightily when he heard the news.

AFTER HIS TORTOISE MOUNTAIN experience, Xuefeng followed in the footsteps of his teacher, Deshan, by withdrawing to a hermitage in his native province of Fujian, but soon he developed ties with the ruler of that province, a man greatly interested in Buddhism. This provincial governor offered Xuefeng financial support, and eventually, in 865, when he was forty-three, Xuefeng settled on Xuefeng Mountain, or Snowy Peak. Although chaos continued to reign in most of the land as the once mighty Tang dynasty disintegrated, the area around Xuefeng Mountain was relatively calm, so that monks, fleeing from persecution in other parts of China, slowly began to move there. Eventually a large monastic community, at times well over fifteen hundred, developed. The fruit of Xuefeng's determination had blossomed and the former "black lacquer bucket" helped many come to awakening, most notably the mighty Yunmen Wenyan (J. Ummon Bun'en), whom we shall meet in the next chapter, and Fayan Wenyi (J. Hogen Bun'eki), the last ancestor covered in this book and Xuefeng's great-grandson in the Dharma.

Life in the monastery on Snowy Peak was austere and teaching was every bit as strict as at Deshan's monastery. Xuefeng did not hesitate to call hapless monks before him "lacquer buckets" and knew how to wield the stick. But it was always for the purpose of helping a student to not get caught in the same traps that had caught him, never as punishment. Once he asked a monk who had come to speak with him where he had come from. When the monk gave the name of the region he had left, Xuefeng asked him whether he had traveled by land or by sea. "Neither route has anything to do with it," the monk replied (echoes of the Flying Ape Mountains). "Well, then," said the master, "how did you get here?" The monk, stubbornly clinging to "emptiness," replied, "Was there anything obstructing my way?" Xuefeng gave him a blow. Wake up! Emptiness is not some separate state—it is the river, it is the land, it is just this.

Another time, the master came to the Dharma hall and lifted his horsehair flywhisk. "This," he said, "is for those who are inferior." A monk asked what he would do for those who are superior. Xuefeng again lifted his *hossu*. "But that was for those who are inferior," the monk said, walking right into the trap. The master struck him. Don't get caught in duality, monk! Don't get caught in the duality created by your mind. What inferior? What superior? Just this raised flywhisk. Wake up!

Xuefeng used blows but he sometimes used them in surprising ways. A high official of the province once gave him a silver chair. One of the monks commented on what a fine gift this was and asked what the master was going to give the official in return. The master put both his hands on the ground and said, "Please strike me lightly." Who knows, perhaps he was tired of ladling out blows. But what a fine teaching about human, dualistic, quid pro quo mentality, is it not? Why not just receive the chair?

Teaching did not always involve blows, for his "black lacquer bucket" years of frustration surely raised empathy in Xuefeng's heart on many occasions. When one has been there, as Xuefeng had, one's understanding of the other's suffering is surely much deeper. "Master! Please express what I cannot express," a monk pleaded. "For the Dharma's sake I have to save you," said Xuefeng and he lifted his horsehair whisk. The monk departed immediately. Did he grasp the teaching? Do you? Another time a newcomer came to him and said, "I have just come to this monastery. I beg you to show me the way to the truth." Xuefeng replied, "I would rather be crushed to dust. I dare not blind any monk's eye." Open your eyes, he might have added. There is no way to be shown, for it can only be lived.

The master was also clear and direct, offering teaching that is easily accessible to twenty-first-century practitioners. Here is an exchange with an overzealous student who obviously thought that more was better. "I'll give you medicine that would revive a dead horse," the master said. "Can you swallow it?" The student, who would later become one of his Dharma heirs, replied that he could. "Then don't bother coming to me [for interviews] many times a day. Just make yourself like a burnt stump on the mountainside. If you put your body or mind at rest for ten years, or maybe seven or even just three, you'll surely discover something." In other words, practice!

Throughout his teaching life, there was a natural give-and-take between the master and his disciples, as demonstrated in a story told by Xuansha Shibei (J. Gensha Shibi), another of Xuefeng's Dharma heirs, after he was a teacher in his own right. Xuansha sent Xuefeng a letter of greeting. The old master opened it in the company of the other monks and found three sheets of paper inside—blank. He asked the monks if they understood. They could not. Xuefeng said, "My prodigal son writes just what I think." When Xuansha heard of this, true Dharma son that he was, he said affectionately, "My old man is in his dotage."

What dotage? "In the future," Yantou had said, "if you want to express great teaching, it must flow out of *you*." Well, it flowed—for forty years. Then one day in the third month of 908, as *The Transmission of the Lamp* tells us, "the Master announced his illness. The General of [Fujian] [he of the silver chair] sent a physician to examine him. The Master said, 'My illness is not an illness.' He declined to take the medicine prescribed for him, but devoted himself to composing a *gatha* for the transmitting of the Dharma." Two months later he died. He was, the record says, eighty-seven. It had been fifty-nine years since he had been ordained.

Fifty-nine years earlier this great heart had set out on a pilgrimage with his bucket, wooden ladle, and culinary skills, determined to realize the Great Matter. On the way he met failure, received many blows, faced endless frustration, and was called many names, chiefly a "black lacquer bucket" of ignorance. He might have been a black lacquer bucket when he set out on his quest, but he was no longer one when he passed away. His tough but deeply compassionate teaching touched countless people, ordained and lay, and thanks to him the Dharma that he so loved lives in us.

What else can we do but make nine bows to this worthy rice cook.

11. YUNMEN

—————————— J. UMMON; 864–949 ——————————

EVERY DAY IS A GOOD DAY

THERE IS A Zen saying that tells us it is the responsibility of each Zen student to stand on the shoulders of his or her teacher. This does not mean a student should strive to be better than the teacher, for in the Zen worldview of "no gain, no loss" (completeness) there can be no "better than." What it means is that the student needs to trust herself, to trust her own voice and so, through necessary years of training under the guidance of a teacher, to express and live the Dharma out of the uniqueness that is her true self. A student who tries to copy a teacher or to express the Dharma only in the teacher's voice is not expressing the Dharma at all but only a secondhand version of another's truth. This is why a skillful teacher is always asking, "How do *you* see it?" with genuine interest in how the student does see it. A Zen teacher never stops learning, and the *dokusan* room is a major source of such learning. Contrary to what Zen students may think, teaching goes in both directions when teacher and student meet.

All the Zen masters covered in this book stood on the shoulders of their respective teachers, none more so than Yunmen Wenyan (J. Ummon Bun'en), who stood on the shoulders of two. He was a giant among the Zen teachers of his day and was, along with Fayan Wenyi (J. Hogen Bun'eki), the last of the truly great masters of Zen's Golden Age.

Yunmen was born in 864 in Jiaxing, which was located between the present-day cities of Shanghai and Hangzhou. As a boy he was able to recite lengthy scriptures from memory and revealed a keen intelligence and a strong pull toward the spiritual life. As Urs App tells us in his fine book *Master Yunmen* (*The Record of Master Yunmen*), the boy "was also characterized by a strong aversion to vulgarity [remember this for later!], a tendency to be exemplary, and great eloquence." He studied for some years under the Vinaya master Zhicheng, leaving the master for some time to take monastic vows at the usual age of twenty, then returning for further study of the Buddhist monastic rule. He became such an adept on the Vinaya that he soon began lecturing on it.

The Vinaya, however, did not seem to fulfill Yunmen's spiritual longings, and so at age twenty-five he traveled to meet a well-regarded Chan teacher named Muzhou Daoming (J. Bokushu Domyo). We first met Muzhou as Huangbo's head monk; it was he who sent the young Linji into Huangbo's interview room to innocently ask his question as to the meaning of Zen. Muzhou was by now an old man who had left monastic life and returned to his ancestral home, where he supported himself and his mother by making sandals. But although he was old, the tough head monk had grown into an even tougher teacher who declined to speak with most of those who sought him. Only the most confident students came to see him. Was Yunmen confident? Perhaps he was simply as determined to awaken as the young Linji had been so many years before. This would make sense since, as we shall see, Yunmen and Linji's temperaments and teaching styles were quite similar.

Here is a description of Yunmen's meeting with Muzhou as recounted in the thirteenth-century text *The Compendium of Five Lamps*. It's another memorable Zen enlightenment story and, although probably embellished somewhat, another powerful reminder of just how much these great Zen masters wanted to awaken and what they were willing to go through in order to realize it.

As Yunmen approached Muzhou's room, he saw the door was open. "I'm in luck," he may have thought—but no such thing. As soon as the elderly master heard him coming, he closed the door. Yunmen persisted. He knocked.

"Who's there?" asked Muzhou.

"It's me." [It's me! Don't all young people think the world revolves around them?]

"What do you want?"

"I'm confused about my life. I would like your instruction, master."

Muzhou opened the door, took one look at Yunmen, and closed it again.

Yunmen was not deterred. He came back the next day but the same thing happened. On the third day, he came again but, this time, he had a plan. When Muzhou opened the door, Yunmen stuck his foot in the opening. He was in!

Muzhou grabbed him and demanded in a loud voice, "Speak, speak!"

When Yunmen began to speak, Muzhou pushed him out the door. "Too late!" he cried out, slamming the door on the young man's foot. The foot broke—and Yunmen awakened!

Yunmen awakened because the extreme pain of that moment forced everything out of his egocentric mind. No more questions, no more confusion, no more seeking instruction, only the intense immediacy of "just this": pain. It is what many of us have experienced in moments of intense crisis, is it not? In those shock-filled moments when we hear of the sudden death of someone we spoke with yesterday, when the doctor delivers an unexpected diagnosis, when our car skids on an icy highway—in those moments don't all our anxieties and worries and confusions, which a minute before had seemed so important, drop off? Are we not, like Yunmen, also left with the immediacy of "just this"? Doesn't Yunmen's awakening resonate with us, we who have had such "just this" moments of our own? Do we recognize them as such and allow them to teach us? Or do we go back to the same old ego-mind churnings once the crisis passes? Yunmen did not go back. Later on, when he was a teacher in his own right, he said to his assembled monks, "Do not miss what this life has to offer, for you will never have another chance. This is no small matter."

YUNMEN STAYED WITH MUZHOU for a few years. Then at some point the elderly Muzhou, realizing perhaps that he was a teacher without a community and in his final days, sent his new Dharma heir to deepen his insight and find support on Snowy Peak with the much younger Master Xuefeng who was by now the most renowned Zen teacher in southern China. Here is the freely adapted record of their meeting as recounted in the Record of Yunmen.

> On his arrival in the village at the foot of Mount Xue, Yunmen ran into a monk.
>
> "Are you going up to Master Xuefeng's monastery today?" he [Yunmen] asked him.
>
> "I am," replied the monk.
>
> "Well, then, please approach the abbot with a question, though you mustn't tell him it's from someone else. Can you do this?"
>
> "Of course," said the monk "What is the question?"
>
> Yunmen explained. "When you arrive, wait until all the monks have gathered to hear the Dharma talk and the master has ascended the Dharma seat. Then approach him and say, 'Hey, old fellow, why don't you get rid of that iron cangue [an iron restraint used on criminals] around your head?'"
>
> The monk agreed to do this [which shows he was either woefully ignorant to think that he could speak to the abbot in this way or that the story was embellished at a later date; no matter—it's a great story].
>
> He carried out his mission. When Xuefeng heard the question, he got down from his seat, grabbed the monk by the chest and shouted, "Speak! Speak!"
>
> The monk could not utter a word.
>
> The master continued. "That question wasn't yours," he said.
>
> "It was mine! It was mine!" [Oh, foolish monk!]
>
> Xuefeng called to his attendant. "Bring me a rope and stick so this rogue can be beaten."

On hearing this, the monk came to his senses. "You are right, master. It was not my question. It was given to me by a monk in the village. He told me what to say."

Xuefeng addressed the assembly. "All of you, go quickly to the village and welcome this worthy monk who will have many disciples."

The next day, Yunmen came up to the monastery. When he came before the master, Xuefeng asked him, "What enabled you to reach this state [of awareness]?"

Yunmen just bowed his head.

The Record tells us, "In this manner did the affinity [between Xuefeng and Yunmen] come about."

The insight of Yunmen's question delivered by the monk can be grasped through the words he spoke the first time he ascended his Dharma seat after later becoming abbot of his own monastery. When the ruler of the province, who was in attendance, bowed and said, "Your disciple asks for your valued teaching," Yunmen replied, "There is nothing special to say. It is better if I don't speak and thereby deceive you all." Words deceive, for they can never fully express that which is unknowable. The unknowable can only be experienced, it cannot be known. Certainly words can partially reveal the truth and must be used in order to communicate and open doorways to true understanding— right thought is, after all, the first step of the Buddha's Eightfold Path of Awakening. But words and knowledge can never express the whole truth. This was the fundamental teaching of the Zen school when its founder opened the door to an "understanding beyond words and scriptures." The imprisoning "iron cangue of Dharma talk" must be removed by Xuefeng, Yunmen was saying. How does he remove it? By being completely aware that his words are indeed only fingers pointing at the moon and not the moon itself. Xuefeng knew this and so did the new arrival at his monastery. This is why the affinity between them arose spontaneously at that first meeting.

How do *we* feel about words and Dharma talks and teachings? Do we see them as skillful means pointing to the truth of who we really are, focused directives that can steer us into possible new ways of seeing and understanding? Do we see them as helpful guides, offering us windows into the depth of insight experienced by those who have come before? There is a paradoxical Zen saying which goes as follows: "We walk the path that no one has trod, following guideposts left by others." Words and talks and teachings are such guideposts but, if we mistake the guideposts for our path (which no one has trod or can ever tread), then we're headed in the wrong direction. For then those words will only deceive, as we seek to gain ego-mind meaning and understanding about that which has no meaning and can never be understood. This is why Zen is not a philosophy, not a metaphysical set of ideas, not even a religion (for religions are based, in part, on doctrines and ego-mind-created ideas). Zen is simply a way—a way of living unattached to anything.

Yunmen studied with Xuefeng for seven years, refining his insight by paring away layers of ego-mind obstructions through the unrelenting skillful means of his teacher. Recall that Xuefeng had said to another monk, "I'll give you medicine that would revive a dead horse. Can you swallow it?" Yunmen could swallow it. He took Xuefeng's medicine just as he had taken Muzhou's, learning to receive whatever the demanding Xuefeng threw at him in order to break down his egocentric, gain-loss mind. It was a harsh world. As Nelson Foster and Jack Shoemaker write in *The Roaring Stream*, "By present-day humanistic standards, the ruthless training he [Yunmen] received under these teachers may seem all wrong, but in medieval Chinese apprenticeships and in Chan study, in particular, it was considered a master's ultimate kindness." Ultimate kindness? Yes, for a skilled master's intent was never to punish, never to humiliate, and never to put down (even though this is what it may seem like today) when he applied extreme techniques in his teaching. The intent of an authentic and enlightened teacher (and let's face it, there were probably some less-than-enlightened teachers who misused this process) was *always* to break down the ego-mind's stubborn insistence on "me," "mine," gain, loss, "better than," "worse than"; to break down the insatiable search for meaning and knowledge and understanding that is the human condition; and to help the student separate from ego-mind, realize its illusory spins on reality, and come face to face with the purity of "just this—as is." This is still the intent of authentic Zen teachers today, but because we live in another age and another culture, the techniques are, of course, different.

Yunmen took Xuefeng's medicine and thrived. It sharpened the discipline he applied to his wandering thoughts, helped him throw off bad habits, honed his awareness of the present moment, and instilled in him teaching skills that were to make him into one of the most demanding Zen teachers who ever lived. After seven years of such intense work, he received Dharma transmission from Xuefeng and became his principal Dharma heir. Yunmen had awakened under Muzhou; under Xuefeng he developed into a masterful teacher who later became a model for those who came after him.

IN HIS LATE THIRTIES, at the dawn of the tenth century, Yunmen left his teacher and set out on a ten-year pilgrimage. This is interesting in light of Yunmen's later railings against pilgrimage. Here is a quote from one of his later Dharma talks given to assembled monks, some of whom were on pilgrimage: "There's a bunch of people who casually gather in groups, manage to quote some sayings of the ancients, try to memorize them, evaluate them with their delusive thoughts, and say: 'I have understood the Buddhist teaching!' They busy themselves with nothing but discussions and while away their days following their whims. Then they come to feel that this does not suit their fancy; they travel through thousands of villages and myriads of hamlets and turn their backs on their parents as well as their teachers. You're acting in just this way, you bunch of rowdies. What is this frantic pilgrimage you're engaged in?" The record tells us that he then chased them out of the hall with his staff.

What is going on here? Why was it all right for Yunmen to go on pilgrimage and not all right for the pilgrim monks? They were different kinds of pilgrimages, is why, their difference based on the intent of the one setting out. Yunmen had studied with two eminent Zen masters, had endured the difficulties of their severe but compassionate methods, and had not flinched. He had awakened, fully realizing that there is nothing to find, nothing to gain, nothing to achieve, and nothing to learn through pilgrimage. Just like the sixty-year-old Zhaozhou (who had passed away only some five or six years earlier at the age of 120, and who had set out on a twenty-year pilgrimage after many years of enlightened living), Yunmen set out on pilgrimage to test and deepen his insight into the "emptiness of all that is" through exchanges with other awakened teachers. His intent was not to find answers, meaning, and direction but rather to reaffirm his inner knowing that there is no direction to be taken. Here is an exchange he had with Zen Master Caoshan when they met as peers:

> YUNMEN: Why is it that one does not know the existence of that which is most immediate?
> CAOSHAN: Just because it *is* the most immediate!
> YUNMEN: Exactly! Exactly!

"That which is most immediate" cannot be known or understood because one already is "that which is most immediate." Just as the eye cannot see itself, the nose cannot smell itself, and the ear cannot hear itself, one cannot know oneself; one can only *be* oneself. Yunmen, on pilgrimage, constantly practiced being himself, for he knew there was nothing outside of himself to find.

Many of the pilgrim monks, on the other hand, were trying to find themselves outside of themselves; they were trying to find their essentialness through reading, discussing, and philosophizing. When for whatever reasons this was not satisfied at one monastery, they simply abandoned their teacher of the moment and set out on pilgrimage again, to find what they were looking for somewhere else, through someone else. Yet "it" cannot be found somewhere else, for "it" is always here—most immediate, most intimate; "it" cannot be realized through someone else because "it" is already oneself. Realizing this is hard work; it is painful because it means letting go of all mental knowledge, all mental certainties, and moving into the scary experience of not-knowing—not knowing anything. Many pilgrims in the tenth century didn't want to do this; they didn't want to hold fast and face the difficult work of dying to ego-self. They much preferred the by-then fashionable route of pilgrimage because they saw that it was much easier. Of course it was easier! It is always easier to dwell in delusion than wake up to reality. "Wake up!" Yunmen thundered, "Go into yourself and investigate thoroughly *on your own* [italics mine]."

All this is hugely instructive teaching for people today who wander from teacher to teacher, from method to method, always looking for something outside of themselves, always following the latest fad, the latest popular teacher, rather than being willing to hunker down and face the painful challenge of realizing that what they are looking for is nothing other than themselves. Sit, practice stilling the ego-mind, and you'll wake up—without ever having to pack a pilgrimage suitcase.

Yunmen traveled around for ten years, primarily in that region of China south of the Yangtze River where so many Zen masters had established their centers. Since both Muzhou's place and Xuefeng's Snowy Peak were located in more distant locations where there were relatively fewer Zen monasteries, it must have exhilarated Yunmen to be able to meet with, meditate with, and sharpen his insight with so many eminent teachers. It's easy to see how this travel could indeed have taken him ten years.

Yunmen visited a number of the teachers of the Caodong (Soto) school, primarily Caoshan, and this is instructive because Yunmen's later teaching style had much more in common with the blows and shouts of the Linji (Rinzai) school, as well as with Shitou's secondary line that came through the brash and severe Deshan. Caodong school teachers were much softer in their teaching methods than their Linji brothers and one wonders if perhaps Yunmen spent a lot of time with them because he was drawn to a softer approach after having spent such an intense period with the blows and shouts.

In the year 911, Yunmen's pilgrimage route took him to the Cantonese region of China in the deep south to visit the temple of the renowned sixth patriarch, Master Huineng, near the city of Shaozhou in Shao Province. He then traveled to Shaozhou, where he met Master Rumin, abbot of Lingshu (Spiritual Tree) Monastery, with whom he developed a deep affinity. Yunmen soon became head monk at Master Rumin's monastery and remained in this position until Rumin's death seven years later. (For those who think that a person who has received Dharma transmission no longer takes on service positions under a Zen master, this example shows otherwise. In modern times, the head monk in the late Koun Yamada Roshi's zendo in Kamakura, Japan, was a roshi, or master teacher, and a former admiral in the Imperial Japanese Navy, to boot.)

What happened next calls for an update on the political situation in China in 918. Eleven years earlier, in 907, the Tang dynasty had officially collapsed, ushering in a period of fifty years known as the Five Dynasties period. In the north, these five dynasties followed one upon the other in quick succession, with chaotic consequences. It was, as the Chinese scholar Ann Paludan writes, "one of the darkest periods in Chinese history." In the south, however, the ten regional kingdoms were more stable, and the Canton region in particular (where Yunmen settled) had become increasingly wealthy, mainly due to its access to the sea through the port of Hong Kong. A man named Liu Yin, who had bravely fought for the central Cantonese government during rebel uprisings and consequently been showered with lofty titles, honors, and riches, eventually became the wealthiest of the wealthy. Wealth brings power, and soon Liu Yin had the whole region under his control. He died in 911, the year that Yunmen arrived, and was succeeded by his brother, Lin Yan. Lin Yan was not satisfied with the titles he had inherited, and soon made himself supreme ruler of the region, conferring upon himself the title of Emperor Gaozu. He called the region Southern Han and it soon became renowned for its cultural and artistic life, since many of the fleeing court officials, poets, and artists of the last Tang court had found refuge there.

Head monk and emperor first met at the funeral ceremonies for Master Rumin in 918, and Emperor Gaozu must have been favorably impressed because he soon called Yunmen in for an audience. He bestowed on him the purple robe reserved for worthy monks and a year later Yunmen was named abbot of Lingshu Monastery, where he had served as head monk under Master Rumin. Imperial recognition, however, had its drawbacks because soon officials, worthy personages, and people of all kinds began coming to the monastery to meet with its abbot whose fame kept growing. Two stone slabs dating from 959 and 964, discovered in 1927, bear inscriptions detailing much of Yunmen's life, telling us, "Master Yunmen got tired of receiving and entertaining people and wished to reside at a remote and pure place." In other words he and his students needed peace and quiet—a feeling we all know well. So in 923, four years after taking up his abbotship, the master went to the emperor and asked his patron if he could move to a quieter spot. The emperor obliged by beginning construction on a new monastery for him on Mount Yunmen. It took five years to complete and in 928 Zen master Yunmen took up residence in Gate of the Clouds Monastery. He was sixty-four years old and would teach there for twenty prolific years until his death.

The extensive body of Yunmen's teaching that has been handed down to us—most of it from this twenty-year period—owes its existence to several factors. First, he led a large and thriving monastic community, during which time he gave many lectures full of eloquence and passion, allowing opportunities for his teachings to be heard by large numbers. Second, his teachings were written down on the spot. The teachings of earlier teachers had been mostly recorded after the masters had passed away but Yunmen's concise, sharp, and pithy teachings were caught in a manner almost like reportage. He did not allow notes to be taken when he spoke but, so the story goes, his attendant dressed himself in paper robes on which he recorded his master's words. One wonders why such a keen-eyed person as Yunmen would not have noticed his attendant dressed in paper and scribbling away furiously, but in the account the attendant in his paper robes was probably meant to represent the numerous monks who surreptitiously took notes during the lectures and after one-to-one exchanges with the master. The irony is that Yunmen, who distrusted words, who had stated at his installation as abbot that "it is better that I don't speak and therefore deceive you all," would be remembered through so many *precise* words. A third factor in the extensive nature of Yunmen's extant teachings is that the teachings were gathered and published within eighty-six years of his death, and they contributed greatly to all three of the major koan collections, *The*

Blue Cliff Record, The Book of Equanimity, and *The Gateless Gate.* These books were compiled in the two hundred years after Yunmen's death and the editors of these collections naturally turned to what was current. It didn't hurt that Yunmen's Dharma great-grandson was the one to compile *The Blue Cliff Record*—the first of the koan collections to be published.

If Yunmen thought that his heavenly majesty Emperor Gaozu would leave him in peace after he had moved to Mount Yunmen, he was mistaken. After a year, the master was called to the imperial palace. Here is the exchange that took place, as handed down in the Record of Yunmen:

> The emperor asked, "What is Chan all about?"
> Master Yunmen said, "Your majesty has the question, and your servant the monk has the answer."
> The emperor inquired, "What answer?"
> Master Yunmen replied, "I request your majesty reflect upon the words your servant has just uttered."

THE EMPEROR WAS PLEASED with this answer, but did he really get it? Was his question answered? What is Zen? "Zen is your question, majesty; Zen is my answer, majesty." That's what Zen is—nothing more. Zen is moment to moment receiving and responding. It is the receiving of questions, words, sounds, smells, heat, cold, actions, situations, and responding accordingly. But in order to respond with "right response," it is essential that one receive without any extra layers created by the discriminating ego-mind. Receive directly and respond directly, over and over again, is the moment-to-moment rhythm of Zen living and Zen practice. This is Zen—always present, always available, always here, always now. There is nothing more. The emperor had received pure Dharma.

Whether he understood it in the Zen way is not clear. He was pleased with the answer, however—so pleased that on the spot he offered Yunmen what he saw as a promotion. He offered him the position of inspector of the monks of the capital. Yunmen's response? Silence. Being inspector of the monks of the capital was the last thing he wanted to do, we can be sure of that. He was human and he had preferences, but he gave a Middle Way response: he didn't say yes, he didn't say no. He stood in silence, allowing the next moment to reveal his path. It did. One of the imperial advisors, who obviously read the situation well, said to the emperor, "The master has completed his training and knows the path; he is not likely to enjoy rising to a high post." The emperor thought for a moment and then turned to Yunmen. "Shall we let you return to your mountain?" he asked. Yunmen jumped for joy and called out three times, "Long live the emperor!" What a relief! He could go back to Gate of the Clouds.

The following day Yunmen was given money, gifts of incense, medicinal herbs, salt, and other goods to take back with him. Later the emperor gave him the title "Genuine Truth," and made donations several times a year—though the Record adds, "these donations were often not duly recorded." Yunmen kept up cordial relations with the imperial court even after the death of Lin Yan in 942. Lin Yan's successor was in power only a year but the succeeding emperor also showered Yunmen with gifts and wrote an imperial inscription for the master's grave.

What to make of all this? It seems to be a far cry from the actions of Bodhidharma who, it will be recalled, did everything he could to keep away from institutional power and patronage. It was a far cry from the many Chan teachers who wanted nothing to do with capital cities, gifts, courts, officials, and emperors. Zhaozhou made officials come to him as he sat down while meeting poor people at the gate; Deshan refused to meet with the governor until tricked into doing so; Xuefeng reciprocated with nothing after receiving a gift of a silver chair. Why was Yunmen so close to seats of power, such a willing receiver of imperial directives and largesse when he so wanted to be set apart and quiet? Why the contradiction?

The answer, it seems to me, is the same as that given to the other obvious contradictions of his life, such as railing against pilgrimage while having been on pilgrimage, and railing against words while speaking lots of them. It lies in these words that he uttered: "He may speak all day but not carry a word in his mouth. He eats and dresses every day, yet it is as if he had neither tasted a grain of rice nor covered himself with so much as a thread." Yunmen is living the "emptiness of all the five conditions," as the Heart Sutra puts it. He goes on pilgrimage knowing there is nothing to find. He gives lectures knowing there is nothing to speak about. He receives a monastery in which to teach, while knowing there is nothing to teach, nobody to teach, and nobody teaching. He accepts gifts of incense, salt, and other goods, while knowing they have no meaning (the reason, perhaps, why they were not duly recorded). He could freely do all this because he was so deeply grounded in his nonexistence. He was such a true *tathagata*, "no-self living," that none of this was a contradiction at all, it was simply the paradox of the Way. Receive directly and respond directly, with nothing added, living free in the Dharma.

YUNMEN TAUGHT ON HIS MOUNTAIN for twenty years and he ran a tight ship. The place was strict and the teaching methods were often severe and harsh, even harsher than those that had led to his own awakening. His severity, however, came of out a passionate desire to shake those in front of him from their delusory state. By the tenth century, Zen had begun to ossify somewhat and, just like Linji before him, Yunmen was determined to bring it back to its roots. The monk practitioners of the tenth century were for the most part riding on the insights of those who had come before them, with little effort (in Yunmen's eyes at least) put into striving to awaken for themselves. Yunmen sought to change that by developing teaching methods to break open his students' ego-minds, methods that became linked to his name.

All his teaching was shaped by an intense, over-the-top energy, and it must have been nerve-wracking to stand in front of him. Students could not hesitate when he asked a question; their response had to spontaneously arise out of their "not-mind" ground rather than from their rational mind. When this did not happen, they were in trouble. Yunmen shouted at them, he beat them, he chased them out of the hall, and he called them names: "country bumpkin," "hick," "numbskull," and "black lacquer bucket" (the latter learned from his own teacher,

Xuefeng). Yunmen's irony and sarcasm may be, Urs App says, "unsurpassed in Chan history." "Come again in thirty years [perhaps you'll be ready then]," he told one seeker. "Then I'll strike you thirty times with my staff." Why? He wanted to awaken them to the "just-this-without-any-ego-mind-interpretation moment." The hit is just a hit; the shout is just a shout; the word is just a word, he teaches his monks and us. Don't get hung up on the discriminating mind's meaning of these things. Receive them as is.

Vulgar language and expression also became one of Yunmen's hallmarks as Zen practitioners who have opened up to koan 21 in *The Gateless Gate* well know: "What is Buddha?" "Shit-stick!" (The question was apparently asked in the monastery latrine, as this was a stick with which people in those days cleaned their bottoms.) His reference to bodily functions was on full display when he stormed up to his teaching platform one day and roared at the assembled monks and guests (everyone had to attend his lectures standing up): "Today I'm getting caught up in words with you: Shit, ash, piss, fire! These dirty pigs and scabby dogs are making their living in a shit pit!" Quite a change from the young man who had a strong aversion to vulgarity. Why? Just like his predecessors Linji and Deshan, he wanted to shock anyone coming to his monastery in order that they might find holiness in the realities of life. Buddha is not anything other than "just this"—even if this is a shit-stick.

One must surely give credit to the many disciples who were willing to endure this seemingly never-ending abuse. But Yunmen did have a softer side during one-to-one times with students. He did, after all, spend time with the successors of the gentle Shitou while on pilgrimage, and the record shows that he didn't always hit and shout:

> "I'm definitely on the wrong track. Please, Master, give me some instruction."
>
> The master said, "What are you talking about?" [What instruction? Live your life.]

He offered engaged, insightful teaching:

Monk: "One should not leave home without one's parents' consent. How would one then be able to leave home?"

The Master said, "Shallow!" [What home?]

The questioner said, "I do not understand."

The Master said, "Deep!" [Of course you don't understand—and that's it!]

He delighted at another's insight:

He said to the assembly, "Every day you come and go, asking endless questions. If you were crossing a river, how would you do so?"

A longtime resident of the monastery replied, "Step."

Yunmen was highly pleased with this answer.

Zen's use of simple, direct responses to questions was raised by the master to a fine art through what came to be known as "Yunmen's one-word barriers":

"What is Chan?" "That's it!"

"What is the most urgent phrase?" "Eat!"

"What is the Way?" "Grab it."

He also used the technique of asking a question and answering it himself—a method, one suspects, born out of the silence that must have often met his questions:

The Master said, "Do you see?"

He answered himself, "I see."

He went on, "What do you see?"

On behalf of those present he replied, "A flower." [Just this.]

Koan 6 of *The Blue Cliff Record* offers another example—and one of Yunmen's most renowned sayings. Once he asked, "I'm not asking about the days before the fifteenth of the month, only about the days after the fifteenth of the month. What have you to say about those days?" He answered his own question, "Every day is a good day." Every day is a good or right day indeed, provided we allow it to unfold by itself.

He did not forget those who came before, however, often taking the teachings of well-known Chan ancestors and adding another layer, as on the occasion when he related the story of Zhaozhou and the breakfast bowl. "I ask for your teaching," a newcomer had asked Zhaozhou. "Have you had your breakfast?" "Yes." "Then go wash your bowl." The monk awakened. Yunmen added, "Tell me: was what Zhaozhou said a teaching or not? If you say it was: what is it that Zhaozhou told the monk? If you say it wasn't: why did the monk in question attain awakening?"

Master Yunmen's teachings were many, varied, and extremely rich, both in insight and teaching methodology. It would be a pity if we let the strict teaching methods of a tenth-century Chinese bodhisattva, concerned only with our awakening, get in the way of what he has to teach us. What can *we* take away from the severe, no-holds-barred approach of a teacher such as this? What stuffing does he have to knock out of us? What urgency does he have to instill in us? What breakdown of "holy, separated-from-reality Zen" does he have to open up for us? What complacency does he have to shake out of us?

Zen Master Yunmen taught at the Gate of the Clouds Monastery for twenty years. The stone inscription tells us that in May 949, when he was eighty-five, he lost his appetite and slept less. He wrote a letter taking his leave of the emperor, wrote instructions that there be no wearing of mourning clothes or funeral ceremony with a carriage or wailing and crying after he had passed away, and he ordered that no monument be built to honor him. On May 10 of that year, he died. The funeral took place fifteen days later and one thousand monks and lay people participated. The sadness of the event is captured in the Record of Yunmen with these poignant words: "On this day the drifting clouds stood [respectfully] still and the grave tree withered. The cry of the mountain's lone monkeys sharpened the pain of the loss, and invisible birds' voices that pierced the woods heightened the regret and sadness of the separation. The mourners hid [their faces] in their collars and stood around crying."

What a tribute to this extraordinary man who continues to teach us to this day. Yunmen's severity and harshness were not remembered, his extreme methods were not remembered, his sarcasms and biting words were not remembered. It was his passion for the truth, his passion to bring his students to awakening, his passion for living in the moment that were remembered that day.

And it was a good day.

12. Fayan

J. HOGEN; 885-958

TWO-HEADED MADNESS: OF WHAT USE IS IT?

WE TEND TO segregate our lives into categories: work life and home life, social life and solitude, intellectual life and "down time," friendships and relationships. Indeed we must do this if we are to navigate a world of differences. But doing so presents a potential trap: if we do not in some way connect these parts of our lives and live them as a whole life, then we run the risk of creating preferences for one part of our life over another. Our segregations can be many, but none is more prone to being segregated than that aspect of our life we call "spirituality." Spirituality, which in our case is the practice of meditation, or Zen, is often seen as something above our everyday life, something better, something removed. We do not easily connect it to everyday living but we must, for if we don't we have missed the boat as to the truth of Zen itself. The practice of Zen is not limited to the meditation mat. The practice of Zen is our entire life and is the very thread that binds our different lives together. Discovering this truth is called awakening, and it can take a circuitous route.

This is what happened to a man named Fayan Wenyi (J. Hogen Bun'eki), a contemporary of Yunmen, both of whose adult lives covered the first half of the tenth century. Fayan was born in 885 near the city of Hangzhou in southern China, just south of today's city of Shanghai, and he entered a monastery at the age of seven. History does not record how this came about. (Did his parents send him? Was he an orphan?) It was the beginning of a spiritual conditioning from which he later had to break free, just as we have to break free from our own particular childhood conditionings. In this monastic setting he grew up to be a highly intelligent, educated young man, keenly interested in reading and exploring the world of ideas and philosophies with a special interest in Confucianism. Eventually, though, he left this monastery and went to another, where he was ordained as a Buddhist monk at the customary age of twenty, and then moved yet again to the city of Maoshan, where he studied the strict rules of the Vinaya. From this he moved to Zen, and began studying with one of Xuefeng's Dharma heirs, Changqing Huileng (J. Chokei Eryo), along the way developing a deep knowledge of the Mahayana Buddhist school known as Yogachara, which taught that all experience is only "mind" and nothing exists outside of this "mind"—a teaching that influenced him greatly.

In all this one discerns a restless spirit, a person seeking to realize the true nature of reality by exploring different paths, different philosophies, different teachers, unable to resolve the Great Matter of life and death but desperately wanting to. In this is he so different from us? Are not our lives also ones of seeking connection to "something other" through different paths, such as work, relationships, children, religion, art, therapy, volunteer work, reading, and spiritual practices? In our spiritual quest, do we not also try this way and that, moving from authority to authority, not satisfied, our questions unanswered? It is the seeker's lot to live this unresolved kind of life, pushing for resolution until, as Zen puts it, resolution is realized and "the box fits the lid." If, however, the seeker gives up in despair, believing that the seeking is too hard, that there is nothing to find, or if the seeker becomes cynical or buys into orthodoxy because it's so much easier to go with the crowd than to struggle alone, then realization cannot arise. Each of us must resolve the Great Matter for ourself, and a basic component of such resolution is not giving up. Fayan did not give up.

When his Zen studies with Changqing didn't lead anywhere, Fayan decided to move on again, undertaking the common pursuit of the day—pilgrimage. He was part of that growing body of monks whom Yunmen would later rail at, for indeed Fayan wanted to understand, to know, and he was prepared to walk until he found a teacher who would give him the metaphysical answers to his metaphysical questions. On his pilgrimage he met other monks with whom he shared the journey, and one can only imagine the conversations among these earnest young men as they walked.

One day, as *The Transmission of the Lamp* tells us, Fayan and his walking companions encountered a huge snowstorm and became lost. Stumbling about, the pilgrimage party came upon a monastery—that of Zen Master Luohan Guichen (J. Rakan Keichin), commonly known as Dizang, Deshan's grandson in the Dharma, who vigorously taught the "here it is" of everything. He once said to a monk, "When you saw me raise the whisk, you bowed and shouted. Why is it that when someone holds up a broom you don't shout in praise?" The traveling monks were warmly welcomed out of the snowstorm and, after they had been fed and their needs taken care of, Fayan went to have a meeting with the master. They had the following exchange:

"Where are you going?" asked Dizang.
"On an ongoing pilgrimage," Fayan replied.
"Why do you go on pilgrimage, monk?"
"I don't know," said Fayan.
"Ah," said the master, "not knowing is most intimate."
Fayan was stopped short, and the record tells us he had a moment of enlightenment.

"Not knowing is most intimate." Not-knowing is closest. The not-knowing Fayan had been trying to eradicate from an early age by constantly seeking to find answers to his questions through different teachers, methods, and knowledge—could that not-knowing actually be the Way? What seemed to open up for Fayan at that moment was a different perspective, a whole new possibility such as opens up for us when we see something with fresh eyes and an open mind. Learning to be aware of such moments and exploring them further is vitally important, for they can be fleeting. This is why regular meetings with a Zen teacher in *dokusan* are so important, for they allow students to speak their insight aloud and thus catch and bring to consciousness new perspectives that are not yet fully realized. Committing to such exploration, however, is not easy.

It was not easy for Fayan. Great doubt came rolling in that night. "What I experienced certainly felt authentic," he might have thought, "but how can I trust it? For I can't *know*. It's so radical! It's so different! How can *not knowing* be the Way? I'm supposed to know and understand. If I don't know, how will I know it's right? How can I be certain?" Isn't that the same doubt that usually assails us whenever we open into a radically new way of seeing? Don't we often do what Fayan probably did during the night—try to grasp the insight with our ego-mind, try to hold on to it and find its meaning? But what happens? We lose the battle. Insight cannot be grasped by the limited ego-mind.

Fayan lost the battle; his desire to know and be certain was too great. The next morning, instead of asking Master Dizang if he could stay and explore this not-knowing further, he chose to reenter his pilgrimage, the snowstorm evidently having abated. He packed up his bundle and joined the other monks at the monastery gate. The kind and courteous Dizang came to say farewell but seems to have had another motive. Having spoken to Fayan the previous evening about Fayan's studies, and possibly sensing that something had been awakened in the young man when he heard the words "not knowing is most intimate," he asked Fayan a further question. Here is how the exchange went, according to the Record of Fayan:

> "Last night," said the master, "I heard you say several times that everything is only mind and the myriad things exist only in the mind. Is that so?"
> "Yes, indeed," replied Fayan.
> "See that boulder lying on the ground? Is that boulder inside or outside the mind?"
> "Inside. It's inside my mind."
> "Well, monk," said the master, "you're going to be carrying around a very heavy boulder as you travel through China."
> Fayan was dumbfounded. He could not answer.

"Please, master, clarify the truth." He put down his bundle and stayed.

A challenging teaching awaits us here in the form of a question. When faced with our own dumbfounded, not-knowing-the-answer moments, do we put down our metaphorical bundles and face the discomfort of the moment in the hope of seeing more clearly, as did Fayan? Or do we withdraw, refuse to face the doubt that has penetrated our certainty, and continue on in the direction we had mapped out for ourselves? This brave moment in the life of Fayan can inspire us when we're faced with our own seeming ignorance, for when faced with such moments we so often want to run away or try to cover up rather than hang in there to face the embarrassment, failure, and even pain of not knowing the answer. Like Fayan we too must stay to face the doubt and fear, we too must stay to face the not-knowing and examine it, for it is only in the not-knowing that our "answer" lies.

This is what Fayan did. He stayed and entered into the life of what was a vibrant monastic community; the year was approximately 911 (around the time that Yunmen began serving as head monk at Master Rumin's place). It was over a century since Baizhang had introduced his monastic rule into the way of Zen, and one can assume that the order of the day in Master Dizang's monastery was the daily rhythm of meditation, Dharma talks, study, work, and private interviews with the master. Fayan took advantage of these interviews, meeting with Dizang every day for a month, bringing with him his conclusions and understanding of philosophical studies and insights. And each time the master would laugh and say, "That's not the buddhadharma at all. That's not it." This happened every day. Zen students know only too well the frustration and anguish that Fayan must have felt each time he went for his interview. It's the same feeling most practitioners experience when they bring some seemingly brilliant insight or "answer" to a koan into the *dokusan* room, only to be told "that's not it." Fayan kept trying harder and harder until one day, probably exhausted after many sleepless nights, he came to Dizang and said, "I have no words to say."

This time Dizang did not laugh or send him away, for he knew Fayan was ready. He knew his student's ego-mind had collapsed, had stilled, and that he could now hear. This is what Master Dizang then said in so many words: "Everything you see, everything you hear, everything you touch and taste and feel and, yes, think, is buddhadharma. *Everything* is buddhadharma, the enlightened state." And at that moment Fayan experienced his great awakening. He was, as Shibayama Roshi puts it, "free in the Dharma thereafter." Eventually he became Master Dizang's Dharma successor.

It is important to remember that Fayan arrived at this moment having spent many years living with the deep insight that everything in the phenomenal world is an illusion—which is true. As the sixth patriarch put it, "Ultimately, not one thing exists." This is foundational Zen teaching, expressed in the Heart Sutra as "the emptiness of all the five conditions"—the emptiness of forms, sensations, conceptions, discriminations, awareness itself. Everything we receive with our senses is not reality but our discriminating ego-mind's version of that reality. When the discriminating mind is still, reality then can be called "empty." This "emptiness" is what Fayan had realized, but it was not the whole truth. As his Dharma ancestor Shitou wrote in the "Identity of Relative and Absolute," "to encounter the absolute [emptiness] is not yet enlightenment." Fayan had realized, before his pilgrimage, that people create their version of reality in the discriminating mind, but he sort of got stuck there—stuck in the realization that form is emptiness or, put another way, that relative is absolute. He hadn't yet gone full circle—hadn't realized that emptiness is form, absolute is relative. He had, however, glimpsed this when Dizang spoke to him about the boulder. Yes, the boulder is in the mind *and* it's real. Having worn out his discriminating mind trying to come up with words to describe his limited view of what buddhadharma is, Fayan's discriminating mind stilled and he could finally hear the truth: that everything is buddhadharma. Absolute is relative, relative is absolute. Everything is mind, mind is everything. Fayan was to teach this for the rest of his life.

Later on, when he was a Zen master himself, Fayan told his students the story of a Zen monk who lived alone in a cottage. Above the door the monk had written the word "mind." Above his window he had written the word "mind." And on the wall he had written the word "mind." Fayan said, "Above the door he should have written 'door.' Above the window he should have written 'window.' On the wall he should have written 'wall.'" Perhaps one could add that the monk could have then erased all the words and just *lived* in the cottage. Relative is relative, yes; absolute is absolute, yes; *and* relative is absolute and absolute is relative. This is the true identity of relative and absolute, so perfectly expressed in Shitou's great poem.

By 907, the once mighty Tang dynasty had finally fallen, to be replaced by a fifty-year period known as the Five Dynasties, described in the previous chapter. The written record indicates that the chaos of this period does not seem to have affected Fayan much, for it was during this time, having completed his studies with Dizang, that he made his way to the independent kingdom of Nantang, whose rulers soon bestowed great honors on him. Here is another example of a Zen master who does not shun connections to power but rather—like Yunmen—uses it as a means to spread the Dharma. (One is reminded of the Buddha's connections to the powerful King Bimbisara, from whom he received, among other favors, gifts of land for his sangha.) Zen Buddhism was now well established in China, and the rulers of Nantang were probably eager to connect themselves with a brilliant man like Fayan. Such relationships teach us that Zen can authentically flourish among seats of power as well as on mountaintops—provided its leaders remain grounded in the Dharma. Later Fayan took over the leadership of Qingliang Monastery in Jinling where, according to *The Transmission of the Lamp*, he had many disciples.

Fayan's education had begun at a very early age and his interest in learning never flagged. He was well read and wrote many works, though most of them have been lost. One major exception is his treatise entitled "Ten Guidelines for Zen Schools," the full text of which can be found in Thomas Cleary's book *The Five Houses of Zen*. It is an important work, well worth exploring, for it lays out strong guidelines for both Zen students and Zen teachers, as applicable today as they were in the tenth century. It shows Fayan to have been an exacting taskmaster who saw through the delusions that can enter the practice of even the most renowned teachers, himself included. Here is what he writes in the preface: "If... people have no experience of the doctrines of the teachings, it is hard to break through discrimination and subjectivity. Galloping right views over wrong roads, mixing inconsistencies into important meanings, they delude people of the following generations and inanely enter into vicious circles. I have taken measure of this, and it is quite deep; *I have made the effort to get rid of it, but I have not fully succeeded.* The mentality that blocks the tracks just grows stronger; *the intellectual undercurrent is not useful* [italics mine]."

This is splendid encouragement, as well as warning for us all, whether teacher or student. It comes from the pen of an intellectual who writes that intellectual understanding "is not useful." He does not do away with doctrines or teachings, but clearly says that what is necessary is the *experience* of these teachings. Without such experiential understanding, an understanding which is beyond words and scriptures, as Huineng taught, right teaching will simply be passed on as empty words—or, as Fayan's incisive metaphor puts it, "right views galloping over wrong roads." Clinging to superficial understanding is very common, he warns us, and we must constantly be on the lookout for it because this "mentality blocks the tracks" and—big warning—it "just grows stronger." It is essential for us to understand that as our Zen practice grows, the work gets simpler but it never gets easier. We are deluded if we believe that we will reach a point where we have "got it" and we can relax and stop practicing. Our practice can never stop, and realizing this is already an awakened moment. When we surrender to the unending nature of practice, paradoxically it becomes far less burdensome, for then we realize that practice is not a means to an end but the end itself.

Here is a brief overview of the "Ten Guidelines." The first guideline reiterates Fayan's view that people are "lazy about pursuing intense inquiry" and concerned only with "hurriedly striving for leadership," thus causing "the current teaching to degenerate." The second guideline decries the factionalism (my way is better than your way) that arises when people "do not realize that the Great Way takes no sides"—a factionalism that sadly seems to pervade to this day in all religions. The next two guidelines return to the central issue of a Zen practitioner's need to be grounded in the Dharma (the "bloodline," Fayan calls it) and to press on until "the source" is realized. He admonishes people who "leave their teacher without any insight of their own," which only results in "their restless consciousness" being "unclear." (Remember that he did not leave Dizang the morning after the snowstorm.) Next Fayan warns teachers that they must first realize for themselves that everything comes from the mind's creations. For "if one cannot eliminate one's own illness, how can one cure the diseases of others?" The sixth and seventh guidelines address students, urging them to find a good teacher, to not rely on their own limited understanding, to penetrate their doubts until there is clarity, to heed the ancestral saying that "only when your view is beyond your teacher can you bring out the teacher's teaching." (This is "standing on the shoulders of your teacher," as the Zen saying goes.) Fayan goes on to thunder, "The stuff of a real man is not for sissies. Don't be a servile literalist...[and] flap your lips and beat your gums. Wisdom comes out in the village of infinite nothingness." This is followed by guideline eight, in which he reiterates the need to be careful not to get stuck in "sectarian methodology" and erudition. "There are many people who...flaunt their eloquence and set forth their wealth of learning like stocks in a storehouse; when they get here, they must be taught to be still and silent, so that the road of speech cannot be extended." In the ninth guideline, Fayan, who, in the tradition of Wang Wei, was an excellent poet, goes after people who call themselves Zen poets but are not, for "they spit out whatever they feel and in many cases their works are...vulgar." This is important, he says, not only for the art of poetry but also because when "you spout vulgarities, you disturb the influence of the Way." In other words, bad Zen poetry is bad Zen. Finally he gives it to the leaders of Zen communities who fail to "exert their strength to continue the Zen teaching...[and to] establish a site of enlightenment," instead "fooling around in cocoons of ignorance...failing to investigate the great matter."

Fayan's closing words bear repeating: "I have exposed these folks to warn people in the future. Meeting with a chance for wisdom is not a small matter; choosing a teacher is most difficult. If you can bear the responsibility [to do this] yourself, eventually you will fulfill maximum potential. I am forcibly dispensing a stunning medicine, willing to be subjected to slander and hatred, so that people on the same path may be assisted in awakening." Quite a statement. He obviously knew he would be attacked but was willing to endure such attacks for the sake of speaking the truth. Can we say the same for ourselves? Are we willing to speak the truth in our sanghas and in our daily life even if it means being subjected to "slander and hatred," even if it means not being liked? Not being liked is one of the most insidious reasons for human inaction, but which is more important—to be liked or to speak the truth? Zen master Fayan obviously chose the latter and as such he is a powerful model of inspiration.

All his life, Fayan's passion was to investigate the Great Matter and because of this he read widely and was exceptionally open to the insights of Buddhist schools other than Zen. Indeed, one of his central teachings was based on the teaching of an early school of Buddhism called Huayen (J. Kegon), whose philosophy greatly influenced the development of Zen. Huayen stated, "All things are in complete harmony with one another, since they are all manifestations of one principle. They are like individual waves of the same sea." In other words, absolute or essential reality is manifest as all things. All things manifest absolute or essential reality. This, it will be recalled, had been a fundamental teaching of Mazu as he sought to clarify the way of Chan some 150 years earlier. Fayan expressed this teaching in the following way: "If you must understand the meaning of buddha nature then just pay attention to what's going on... If you miss the opportunity, then that is 'passing your days and nights in vain.' If you spend your time trying to understand form in the middle of nonform...you are missing your opportunity. So, do we therefore say that we should realize nonform in the midst of form? Is that right? If your understanding is like this, then you're nowhere near it. You're just going along with the illness of two-headed madness. Of what use is it? All of you, just do what is appropriate for the moment. Take care!"

"Two-headed madness." What a powerful way to describe our mind's unrelenting insistence on separating everything into this or that, absolute or relative, spirit or world. When one fully realizes the nonseparation or harmony of all that exists, then all things are always complete. This is why Zen is practiced not only in the zendo but is our very life, where practice never ceases. Recall Zhaozhou's words: "From the practice hall you have come, from the practice hall you shall go." Every moment is the practice hall; every moment is the practice of meditation. If you sit in the emptiness of a spiritual bubble, separated from the world (which is where Fayan lived for many years before his awakening), you are a ghost. And if you live in the world believing that it is the whole of reality, you are equally a ghost. This is two-headed madness, and transcending this madness is the work of Zen.

Fayan expressed this teaching brilliantly and spontaneously in the episode of two monks and the bamboo blind handed down to us as koan 26 in *The Gateless Gate* and koan 27 in *The Book of Equanimity*. A monk came to Master Fayan's room for instruction, and the master kindly gave it. He pointed to an unrolled bamboo blind covering a window. The two monks who were attending to him went to raise it, each doing exactly the same action. Fayan said, "One has it, and one has not." This was the extent of the instruction—though we're not told whether the questioning monk got it or not.

This statement by Fayan could certainly be viewed as a biased judgment on his part. After all, the two monks both did exactly the same job, yet one seems to be judged as having done a good job and the other a bad job. "That's not fair!" we would probably say, for we navigate this world of judgment every day: so-and-so is better than or worse than, promoted or demoted, got the job or didn't get the job, got the praise or didn't get the praise. This is the way of the relative world and it brings suffering and pain, for it is the world of comparisons and differences— me against you. Such suffering, Fayan tells us, is a delusion. It can be transcended. But how?

We can't do it by thinking about it. In the relative world, *this* is always in opposition to *that*, but trying to transcend such opposition through the ego-mind is not possible, for oppositions are the creations of that very mind. Oppositions and differences can only be transcended when the ego-mind is still and when differences, separations, comparisons, and judgments drop off, because a still mind cannot differentiate. For a still mind, there is only oneness, and in oneness what can you possibly have or not have? What can you possibly gain or lose? Who can you possibly "be against"? But, while this is true, it is also true that world of differences *does* exist. So there are those who *do* have and those who do *not* have, those who gain and those who lose, those who get the promotion and those who don't; those who get the praise and those who don't. Fayan teaches that to transcend this world of differences, *while fully living it*, we must realize the *emptiness* of such differences. So, when you have something—a job, a title, approval—don't be fooled. You don't have anything, for there is nothing to have! Conversely, when you *don't have*—the job, the title, the approval, and so forth—don't be fooled, for there is nothing to *not* have! "Have" and "have not" are equally empty.

If both monks who rolled up the blind were awake to the true nature of reality (that is, its emptiness), they would continue serenely rolling up the blind, no matter what the master said. If they were not awake, they could easily view themselves as having been judged, see themselves in opposition to each other, and suffer. If you are awake to the true nature of reality, you will serenely continue living your life, no matter how your life is viewed, judged, or named, not bothered by having or not having, just living, responding to each moment as it arises. If you are not awake, two-headed madness will catch you and you will suffer.

Master Fayan was constantly on the lookout for two-headed madness, not only in the lives of his students but also in his own life, because "the mentality that blocks the tracks just grows stronger." It's the reason why he was so fierce in his protection of the Dharma and its disciplines. His teaching style, however, was not fierce at all. As Dumoulin tells us, "Many disciples...entrusted themselves to his sure and gentle guidance. His psychological insight and clever versatility were widely reputed...While he did not pounce upon his students and strike them with his staff, he did give them answers of extraordinary precision and power." Fayan had over a thousand disciples at Qingliang Monastery, and they obviously flocked to him because they saw that he was the real thing. His teaching, with its emphasis on "same" and "different," came to be known as the Fayan school, one of the Five Schools of Zen. It was to impact Zen not only in China but particularly as it moved overland into Korea.

Master Fayan had sixty-three Dharma heirs. Some of them became renowned teachers themselves. He headed a monastery and a Zen school was even named after him. Yet the school died out after a few generations. How apt! How right! For Zen itself must die.

Epilogue

WHAT HAPPENED NEXT? The death of Yunmen in 949 and nine years later the death of Fayan marked the close of Zen's Golden Age—that period of some three hundred years during which Zen emerged as a distinctive Buddhist sect. The close of this chapter in Zen history coincided with the dawn of the Song dynasty emperors, family members descended from officials in the Beijing area, who came to power in 960 and ushered in a rule of some three hundred years of stability, prosperity, and unexcelled intellectual and artistic development. As Ann Paludan puts it, "the scholar's [calligraphy] brush replaced the warrior's steed." The Song emperors not only brought to an end the chaos of the Five Dynasties period but also the preceding turbulence of the dying years of the mighty Tang dynasty which, it will be recalled, began its downward descent in 755—right at the time when Mazu and Shitou had embarked on their teaching paths.

Zen dawned and flourished creatively during unsettled times. When stability and prosperity took hold, organization and methodology began to predominate. This had many benefits. The publication of koan collections allowed the in-depth, spontaneous teaching of the early Zen ancestors to be introduced to far more people than ever before; instead of the seeker walking around China to find a teacher, the teacher came, so to speak, to the seeker. The formation of the Five Schools of Zen, which were created a long time after the deaths of their founders, helped Chan practitioners more easily trace the development of the Dharma. And the emphasis on fine arts during this time encouraged the development of Chan calligraphy, painting, and poetry, adding to the expansion of the expression of Chan and its appeal. All told, as Urs App writes, during this period Chan "broadened its influence dramatically and grew into a considerable force both religiously and culturally." The institutionalization of Chan during the Song dynasty years, however, smothered some of Zen's iconoclastic and inventive character—an inevitable result of such a development. Perhaps it is why we call those previous free-for-all years spanning the mid-seventh to the mid-tenth centuries Zen's golden years.

Chan flourished in China until the twelfth and thirteenth centuries, after which it slowly diminished in scope and influence there. Around this time two Japanese monks, Myoan Eisai and Eihei Dogen, traveled to China to study the Way with some of its eminent teachers and subsequently brought the essence of Chan to the shores of Japan. In Japan, the word *chan* became *zen* and eventually all of the Chinese ancestors received Japanese names, which is how some Zen students in the West know them today. Countless books have been written for Westerners about Japanese Zen (for Japan is the country with which Westerners tend to associate Zen). One of them, Heinrich Dumoulin's comprehensive *Zen Buddhism: A History, Japan*, gives a fine overview of its developments in that country. Japan, however, was not the first country to see the spread of the new sect beyond China's borders: Chan moved to Korea from China in the seventh century and continues to be a strong religious influence in that country to this day.

In the twentieth century, Japanese Zen traveled to the West through such pioneers as the scholar D. T. Suzuki and Rinzai teachers like Joshu Sasaki Roshi and Soen Nakagawa Roshi. Shinryu Suzuki Roshi and Taizan Maezumi Roshi of the Soto lineage also opened Zen centers in the United States, while Master Seung Sahn and his Kwan Um school of Zen firmly rooted the Korean Zen heritage in the West. For those seeking an overview of Zen in the West, one could do no better than James Ishmael Ford's book *Zen Master Who? A Guide to the People and Stories of Zen*.

What would the Chinese Zen ancestors have said about all this?

Would they have been surprised? Perhaps not. After all, they had unbridled confidence in the mysterious movement of the Dharma. But we are not surprised because we are able to look back on their insightful, demanding, and above all creative teaching and see that taken as a whole it is extraordinary. Our debt to these masters is unbounded.

We also owe a great debt to another group of people from Zen's Golden Age—those countless, anonymous men (and some women) whom we know as the generic monks who asked questions only to receive a blow, a shout, a put-down, or a perplexing answer that made no sense. We know them as "a monk asked" or "a monk said," and often forget that they were people who had their own personal histories, deep longings, different personalities, and unique reasons for entering the difficult monastic way of Zen. Some of them stayed at their monasteries and awakened, becoming distinguished teachers themselves; some of them stayed and awakened, remaining content with being rice cooks; some of them stayed and went to their grave still perplexed; some of them left and became farmers or moved to the cities; some of them left and served the imperial court; some of them left and got into trouble; some of them left and took up another spiritual path.

No matter what eventually happened to them, whether they stayed or not, these monks must have been changed, no matter how short a time they had spent in the presence of their Zen masters. For it must have changed them to stand dumbfounded in front of one of Yunmen's one-word barriers, to talk of their angst with the compassionate Shitou in his hermitage, to have tea with the 110-year-old Zhaozhou, or to receive thirty blows from the unrelenting Deshan. It must have changed them to hear Linji's shocking words "kill the buddha," to meet the inventive Guishan in the kitchen and be stumped by his questions, or to be deafened by the mighty roar of a larger-than-life Mazu. It must have changed them because Zen changes one, no matter whether one practiced in the ninth century or practices today. For when you practice Zen and stick with it, you begin to see the world with different eyes. Zen changes you, and that is what these monks sensed Zen had to offer, that is why they traveled miles to find a teacher, and that is why so many of them endured. And it is because of this teacher-student relationship that we practice today. A teacher, no matter how creative or insightful, cannot be a teacher without students. Teacher and student together express the teaching—both then and now—and pass it on. This is why these anonymous monks need to be honored by us, need to be thanked, just as much as their extraordinary teachers do.

But how do we thank them? How do we thank our Zen Chinese ancestors? What do we say? We don't say anything. The best tribute we can give them is surely the one they would have wanted. "Make the Dharma your own," is what they say to us. "Practice, don't give up, and trust yourself, for the Dharma lives on as you."

ACKNOWLEDGMENTS

ALTHOUGH IT HAD been suggested by a few of my Zen students over the years that my talks on the Chinese ancestors be turned into a book, the idea seemed so out of the realm of possibility that I never really gave it further thought. It was only when my very determined daughter, Caroline Kishin Abels, began a persuasive campaign to make me change my mind that I began to open up to the idea. A professional writer and editor, as well as my (very serious) Zen student, Carrie assured me that she would transcribe my talks and help me shape them into written form—which is exactly what she did. In the process, her innate editorial talents, as well as her developing Zen insight, helped me to correct my literary efforts and catch those places where my Zen expression was not clear. My gratitude to her is unbounded.

Great thanks also to Sensei Gregory Hosho Abels, my husband of forty-four years and co-resident teacher at Still Mind Zendo. Greg's support and encouragement has been unswerving throughout the process of writing this book, and his deep grasp of the Dharma gave me great confidence that whenever he OK'd a chapter, paragraph, or phrase, it was, indeed, correct expression of Zen. Likewise, gratitude to my teacher, Roshi Robert Jinsen Kennedy, to whom I owe so much, and who so skillfully guided me in my formative years of Zen training. There was no way I would have submitted this manuscript if Roshi had not given it a thorough examination and I am deeply grateful for his attention to detail as he offered his comments.

The members of my sangha, Still Mind Zendo in New York City and its affiliate in Pittsburgh, Plum Blossom Zendo, are also owed a great debt of gratitude. Their genuine reception of my talks over the years gave me courage to embark on this process, and their encouragement as I was writing the book has been truly heartwarming. Special thanks to sangha members Cynthia Zuyiu Brown and Jean Seiwa Gallagher for their helpful assistance with additional editing, Frank Mu Shin Lo Cicero for creating the lineage chart, and Bruce Sengan Kennedy for his guidance on the technical aspects of publishing.

Looking outside my immediate family and Zen family, I owe great thanks to Andy Ferguson, whose knowledge of these Chinese ancestors is remarkable. Andy not only provided me with the fine map in this book but also corrected all my Chinese province names and, above all, introduced me to new information about Bodhidharma that is being discovered by scholars. Deep thanks also to Roshi Gerry Shishin Wick, my colleague in the White Plum Asanga, who so generously gave of his time by reading the manuscript and offering insightful comments.

Finally, great gratitude to my Wisdom editor, Josh Bartok, whose encouragement, extremely kind editorial comments, and helpful technical support made the whole process seem, after all, quite simple.

APPENDIXES

This map of China shows the geographical locations associated with the ancestors profiled in this book.

LINEAGE CHART

This simplified lineage chart traces only the dharma relationships among the twelve Zen masters in this book. All of the masters had dharma successors in addition to the ones listed here, and the official Zen lines, of course, have numerous other teachers.

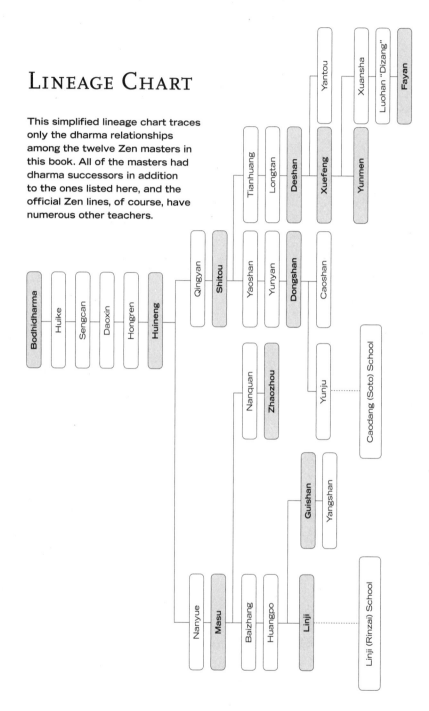

SOURCES

CHAPTER 1: BODHIDHARMA

Sources include Red Pine's *The Zen Teaching of Bodhidharma*, Ferguson's "Did Bodhidharma Exist and Did He Meet Emperor Wu?," Sekida's *Two Zen Classics: Mumonkan, Hekiganroku*, Dumoulin's *Zen Buddhism: A History, India and China*, Yamada's *Gateless Gate*, and Cleary and Cleary's *The Blue Cliff Record*. The rendering of case 1 from *The Blue Cliff Record* is my own.

CHAPTER 2: HUINENG

Sources include Ferguson's *Zen's Chinese Heritage*, Cleary's *Transmission of Light* and *The Sutra of Hui-neng*, Yampolsky's *The Platform Sutra of the Sixth Patriarch*, Mu Soeng's *The Diamond Sutra*, and Yamada's *Gateless Gate*.

CHAPTER 3: MAZU

Sources include Cheng Chien's *Sun Face Buddha: Record of Ma-tsu*, Dumoulin's *Zen Buddhism: A History, India and China*, Sutherland's "Koans for Troubled Times," Paludan's *Chronicle of the Chinese Emperors*, Ferguson's *Zen's Chinese Heritage*, Sekida's *Two Zen Classics: Mumonkan, Hekiganroku*, and Muller's translation of the *Dhammapada*.

CHAPTER 4: SHITOU

Sources include Cleary's *Book of Serenity,* Leighton and Wu's *Cultivating the Empty Field,* Ferguson's *Zen's Chinese Heritage,* Dumoulin's *Zen Buddhism: A History, India and China,* Sutherland's "Koans for Troubled Times," Burger's *Amongst White Clouds,* and O'Connor and Johnson's *Where the World Does Not Follow.* The translations of "The Identity of Relative and Absolute" and the Heart Sutra are by Taizan Maezumi and Bernie Tetsugen Glassman, with further reworking by Glassman and Peter Muryo Matthiessen.

CHAPTER 5: GUISHAN

Sources include Ferguson's *Zen Chinese Heritage,* Chung-Yuan Chang's *Original Teachings of Chan Buddhism,* Heine and Wright's *Zen Classics,* Ichimura's translation of *The Baizhang Zen Monastic Regulations,* Cleary's *Sayings and Doings of Pai-chang,* Foster and Shoemaker's *The Roaring Stream,* Paludan's *Chronicle of the Chinese Emperors,* Collcutt's *Five Mountains,* Aitken's *The Mind of Clover,* Diener, Ehrhard, and Fischer-Schreiber's *The Shambhala Dictionary of Buddhism and Zen,* and Cleary's *The Five Houses of Zen.* The rendering of Koan 40 from Yamada's *Gateless Gate* is my own, as is case 15 from Wick's *The Book of Equanimity.*

CHAPTER 6: LINJI

Sources include Wick's *The Book of Equanimity,* Dumoulin's *Zen Buddhism: A History, India and China,* Watson's *The Zen Teachings of Master Lin-chi,* and Paludan's *Chronicle of the Chinese Emperors.*

CHAPTER 7: ZHAOZHOU

Sources include Green's *The Recorded Sayings of Zen Master Joshu,* Watson's *The Zen Teachings of Zen Master Lin-chi,* Yamada's *Gateless Gate,*

Foster and Shoemaker's *The Roaring Stream*, Mitchell's *Tao te Ching*, Ferguson's *Zen's Chinese Heritage*, and Benn's *China's Golden Age*. The information about Mozart is from Roger Norrington in the 2010 documentary *In Search of Beethoven*.

CHAPTER 8: DONGSHAN

Sources include Ferguson's *Zen's Chinese Heritage*, Powell's *The Record of Tung-shan*, Chung-Yuan Chang's *Original Teachings of Chan Buddhism*, and Dumoulin's *Zen Buddhism: A History, India and China*.

CHAPTER 9: DESHAN

Sources include Ferguson's *Zen's Chinese Heritage*, Yamada's *Gateless Gate*, Cleary and Cleary's *The Blue Cliff Record*, and Shibayama's *The Gateless Barrier*. The Proust quote is from *In Search of Lost Time, Vol. II: Within a Budding Grove*, Moncrieff and Kilmartin, translators.

CHAPTER 10: XUEFENG

Sources include Cleary and Cleary's *The Blue Cliff Record*, Foster and Shoemaker's *The Roaring Stream*, Chung-Yuan Chang's *Original Teachings of Chan Buddhism*, Ferguson's *Zen's Chinese Heritage*, and Powell's *The Record of Tung-shan*. The Basho poem is my rendering of a translation in Hamill's *Narrow Road to the Interior and Other Writings*.

CHAPTER 11: YUNMEN

Sources include Cleary and Cleary's *The Blue Cliff Record*, App's *Master Yunmen*, Ferguson's *Zen's Chinese Heritage*, Chung-Yuan Chang's *Original Teachings of Chan Buddhism*, Foster and Shoemaker's *The Roaring Stream*, Paludan's *Chronicle of the Chinese Emperors*, and Dumoulin's *Zen Buddhism: A History, India and China*.

CHAPTER 12: FAYAN

Sources include Ferguson's *Zen Chinese Heritage,* Cleary and Cleary's *The Blue Cliff Record,* Shibayama's *The Gateless Barrier,* Paludan's *Chronicles of the Chinese Emperors,* Foster and Shoemaker's *The Roaring Stream,* Armstrong's *Buddha,* Cleary's *The Five Houses of Zen,* Diener, Ehrhard, and Fischer-Schreiber's *The Shambhala Dictionary of Buddhism and Zen,* and Dumoulin's *Zen Buddhism: A History, India and China.*

EPILOGUE

Sources include Paludan's *Chronicle of the Chinese Emperors,* Dumoulin's *Zen Buddhism: A History, Japan,* App's *Master Yunmen,* and Ford's *Zen Master Who?*

BIBLIOGRAPHY

Aitken, Robert. *The Mind of Clover.* New York: North Point, 1984.

App, Urs, trans. and ed. *Master Yunmen.* New York: Kodansha America, 1994.

Armstrong, Karen. *Buddha.* New York: Viking Penguin, 2001.

Benn, Charles. *China's Golden Age.* New York: Oxford University Press, 2002.

Burger, Edward A. *Amongst White Clouds.* Canada: Cosmos Pictures, 2005.

Cheng Chien, trans. *Sun Face Buddha: Record of Ma-tsu.* Fremont, CA: Jain Publishing, 1992.

Chung-Yuan Chang, trans. *Original Teachings of Chan Buddhism.* New York: Pantheon Books, 1969.

Cleary, Thomas, trans. *Book of Serenity: One Hundred Zen Dialogues.* Boston: Shambhala, 1998.

———. *The Five Houses of Zen.* Boston: Shambhala, 1997.

———. *Sayings and Doings of Pai-Chang, Chan Master of Great Wisdom.* Los Angeles: Center Publications, 1978.

———. *The Sutra of Hui-neng, Grand Master of Zen, with Hui-neng's Commentary on the Diamond Sutra.* Boston: Shambhala, 1998.

———. *Transmission of Light: Zen in the Art of Enlightenment by Zen Master Keizan.* San Francisco: North Point, 1990.

Cleary, Thomas, trans., and J. C. Cleary, trans. *The Blue Cliff Record.* Boston: Shambhala, 1992.

Collcutt, Martin. *Five Mountains: The Rinzai Zen Monastic Institution in Medieval Japan.* Cambridge, MA: Harvard University Press, 1981.

Diener, Michael S., Franz-Karl Ehrhard, and Ingrid Fischer-Schreiber. *The Shambhala Dictionary of Buddhism and Zen.* Translated by Michael H. Kohn. Boston: Shambhala, 1991.

Dumoulin, Heinrich. *Zen Buddhism: A History, India and China.* New York: Macmillan, 1994.

———. *Zen Buddhism: A History, Japan.* New York: Macmillan, 1990.

Ferguson, Andy. "Did Bodhidharma Exist and Did He Meet Emperor Wu?" South Mountain Tours, 2010. http://www.southmountaintours.com/pages/Bodhidharma_theory/on_Bodhidharma.pdf (accessed December 30, 2010).

———. *Zen's Chinese Heritage.* Boston: Wisdom Publications, 2000.

Foster, Nelson, and Jack Shoemaker. *The Roaring Stream: A New Zen Reader.* Hopewell, NJ: Ecco Press, 1996.

Ford, James Ishmael. *Zen Master Who? A Guide to the People and Stories of Zen.* Boston: Wisdom Publications, 2006.

Green, James. *The Recorded Sayings of Zen Master Joshu.* Boston: Shambhala, 2001.

Hamill, Sam. *Narrow Road to the Interior and Other Writings.* Boston: Shambhala, 1998.

Heine, Stephen, and Dale S. Wright, eds. *Zen Classics: Formative Texts in the History of Zen Buddhism.* New York: Oxford University Press, 2006.

Hinton, David. *Mountain Home.* New York: New Directions, 2005.

Ichimura, Shohei, trans. *The Baizhang Zen Monastic Regulations.* Berkeley: Numata Center for Buddhist Translation and Research, 2006.

Leighton, Taigen Dan, and Yi Wu, trans. *Cultivating the Empty Field: The Silent Illumination of Zen Master Hongzhi.* North Clarendon, VT: Tuttle Publishing, 2000.

Mitchell, Stephen, trans. *Tao te Ching.* New York: HarperCollins, 1988.

Mu Soeng. *The Diamond Sutra: Transforming the Way We See the World.* Boston: Wisdom Publications, 2000.

Muller, Max, trans. *Dhammapada.* Woodstock, VT: Skylight Paths Publishing, 2002.

Phil Grabsky. *In Search of Beethoven*. Brighton, England: Seventh Art Productions, 2010.

O'Connor, Mike, and Steven R. Johnson. *Where the World Does Not Follow*. Boston: Wisdom Publications, 2002.

Paludan, Ann. *Chronicle of the Chinese Emperors*. London: Thames and Hudson, 1998.

Powell, William F., trans. *The Record of Tung-shan*. Honolulu: Kuroda Institute, University of Hawaii Press, 1986.

Proust, Marcel. *In Search of Lost Time, Vol. II: Within a Budding Grove*. Translated by C. K. Scott Moncrieff and Terence Kilmartin. New York: Random House, 1998.

Red Pine, trans. *The Zen Teaching of Bodhidharma*. New York: North Point, 1987.

Sekida, Katsuki. *Two Zen Classics: Mumonkan, Hekiganroku*. New York: Weatherhill, 1977.

Shibayama, Zenkei. *The Gateless Barrier: Zen Comments on the Mumonkan*. Boston: Shambhala, 1974.

Sutherland, Joan. "Koans for Troubled Times." *Buddhadharma*, Spring 2008.

Wallis, Glenn. "Gautama vs. the Buddha." *Buddhadharma*, Winter 2009.

Watson, Burton, trans. *The Zen Teachings of Master Lin-Chi: A Translation of the Lin chi lu*. New York: Columbia University Press, 1999.

Wick, Shishin Gerry. *The Book of Equanimity: Illuminating Classic Zen Koans*. Boston: Wisdom Publications, 2005.

Yamada, Koun, trans. *Gateless Gate*. Tucson: University of Arizona Press, 1990.

Yampolsky, Philip B., trans. *The Platform Sutra of the Sixth Patriarch: The Text of the Tun-Huang Manuscript*. New York: Columbia University Press, 1967.

About the Author

JANET JIRYU ABELS is the founder and now co-resident teacher, with Gregory Hosho Abels, of Still Mind Zendo in New York City, and the guiding teacher of Plum Blossom Zendo in Pittsburgh. She received Dharma Transmission as a Soto Zen teacher in the White Plum lineage of Taizan Maezumi Roshi in 2000. She is a certified Bio-Spiritual Focusing teacher, and is a member of the White Plum Asanga, the American Zen Teachers Association, and the Lay Zen Teachers Association.

About Wisdom Publications

Wisdom Publications is dedicated to offering works relating to and inspired by Buddhist traditions.

To learn more about us or to explore our other books, please visit our website at www.wisdompubs.org.

You can subscribe to our e-newsletter or request our print catalog online, or by writing to:

Wisdom Publications
199 Elm Street
Somerville, Massachusetts 02144 USA

You can also contact us at 617-776-7416 or info@wisdompubs.org.

Wisdom is a nonprofit, charitable 501(c)(3) organization and donations in support of our mission are tax deductible.

Wisdom Publications is affiliated with the Foundation for the Preservation of the Mahayana Tradition (FPMT).